THE POLITICAL EXECUTIVE
POLITICIANS AND MANAGEMENT IN
EUROPEAN LOCAL GOVERNMENT

The Political Executive

POLITICIANS AND MANAGEMENT IN EUROPEAN LOCAL GOVERNMENT

Edited by
RICHARD BATLEY
and
ADRIAN CAMPBELL

LONDON AND NEW YORK

First published 1992 by
Frank Cass & Co. Ltd

2 Park Square, Milton Park, Abingdon, Oxon OX14 4RN
711 Third Avenue, New York, NY 10017, USA

*Routledge is an imprint of the Taylor & Francis Group,
an informa business*

First issued in paperback 2016

Copyright © 1992 Taylor & Francis

All rights reserved. No part of this book may be reprinted or reproduced or utilised in any form or by any electronic, mechanical, or other means, now known or hereafter invented, including photocopying and recording, or in any information storage or retrieval system, without permission in writing from the publishers.

Notice:
Product or corporate names may be trademarks or registered trademarks, and are used only for identification and explanation without intent to infringe.

British Library Cataloguing in Publication Data

Political Executive: Politicians and
Management in European Local Government
    I. Batley, Richard   II. Campbell, Adrian

    ISBN 978-0-7146-3480-7 (hbk)
    ISBN 978-1-138-97876-8 (pbk)

Library of Congress Cataloging-in-Publication Data

The Political executive : politicians and management in European local government / edited by Richard Batley and Adrian Campbell.
    p. cm.

    First appeared in a special issue of Local government studies, vol. 18, no. 1 (Spring 1992).
    Includes index.
    ISBN 0-7146-3480-8
    1. Local government—Europe. I. Batley, Richard, II. Campbell, Adrian   III. Local government studies.
JS3000.4.A1P65   1992
352.04—dc20   92-4377
                                                          CIP

This group of studies first appeared in a Special Issue of Local Government Studies, Vol. 18, No. 1 (Spring 1992), [The Political Executive: Politicians and Management in European Local Government].

Typeset by Regent Typesetting

Contents

Notes on Contributors — vii

Introduction — 1

The Internal Management of Local Authorities in Britain: The Challenge of Experience in Other Countries   JOHN STEWART — 5

'Aldermen into Ministers': Oslo's Experiment with a City Cabinet   HARALD BALDERSHEIM — 18

Recent Trends in the Relationship between Politics and Administration in Local Government: The Case of Sweden   STIG MONTIN — 31

Constitutional Reform of Local Government in Germany: The Case of North Rhine–Westphalia (NRW)   DIETER GRUNOW — 44

The Relationship Between the Political and the Executive Structure in Italian Local Government   GIANCARLO ROLLA — 59

European Influence on Local Self-Government?   COLIN CRAWFORD — 69

Index — 86

Notes on Contributors

Harald Baldersheim is Professor of Public Administration at the University of Bergen. He is currently on secondment to the Norwegian Centre for Research in Organization and Management. He has been the Director of the research programme evaluating the Norwegian free commune experiments (1987–1991). He has written books and articles on Nordic local government and has also contributed to publications from the international 'Fiscal Austerity and Urban Innovation' project.

Richard Batley is a Reader in Development Administration at the School of Public Policy, University of Birmingham. He has conducted research and consultancies on the policies and administration of urban policy in several Latin American, Asian and African countries as well as in Britain. His most recent publications include *Local Government in Europe: Trends and Developments* (Macmillan, 1991), co-edited with Gerry Stoker.

Adrian Campbell is a lecturer in the Institute of Local Government Studies, University of Birmingham. He has conducted research into local government, provided consultancy services to companies, institutes, and a wide range of local authorities, and has spoken at conferences in Europe and the UK. His most recent publications include *New Technology Skills and Management* (Routledge 1992), co-authored with M. Warner.

Colin Crawford is a senior lecturer in the Faculty of Law at the University of Birmingham, having previously taught in the Universities of Edinburgh, Reading, and Manchester. He has conducted a number of funded research projects in relation to the discretionary powers of local government, and published widely in the fields of local government and planning law. He is also a member of the editorial panel of *Local Authority Law* (Sweet & Maxwell).

Dieter Grunow is Professor of Political Science and Public Administration at the University of Duisberg. He has undertaken research on German public institutions, his main focus being on the relationship between citizens and public institutions. During recent years he has been a consultant to local governments, to the Ministry of the Interior (Bonn), to the OECD, and to voluntary organizations. His publications include *Burgernahe Verwaltung* (Frankfurt, 1988) and a contribution to *The Public Sector* (Berlin, 1991).

Stig Montin teaches political science at Örebro University, Sweden. His area of expertise includes public policy and administration and organization theory. He is engaged in research on local government development and central–local government relations. He is currently finishing his doctoral dissertation.

Giancarlo Rolla is Dean of the Faculty of Economics and Banking and Professor of Public Law at the University of Siena (Italy). He is also Director of the School of Public Administration at the University. He has published books and articles on local government and *a Manuale di diritto degli enti locali* (Rimini, 1992)

John Stewart is Professor of Local Government in the Institute of Local Government Studies, University of Birmingham. He was appointed to the Institute in 1966 to launch management courses for local government officers and was director of the Institute from 1976 to 1983. He is currently Head of the School of Public Policy, which includes the Institute and other departments concerned with the public sector at home and overseas. He has written extensively on the case for local government and on its management.

Introduction

RICHARD BATLEY and ADRIAN CAMPBELL

Having drastically altered local government's powers and finances, the last British Government (1987–92) inaugurated a review of its internal management. This volume, based on a special issue of the journal *Local Government Studies*, takes up a leading issue in that review: the structure and role of the political executive. It does so by reference to examples from Norway, Sweden, Germany, and Italy. We would argue that the possibility of referring to Europe rather than to the English-speaking world for models of reform is not sufficiently exploited. While British local government is in several respects still highly distinct, it is increasingly having to respond to the same external environment as other European local government systems. Moreover, the countries selected for this volume all, to some degree, share with Britain a more collective style of political leadership. The economic and political changes currently underway in both eastern and western Europe are encouraging a reappraisal of all aspects of the role of sub-national government.

With liberalization in the East and economic unification in the West, local government is increasingly exposed to processes emanating in the wider political economy. The consolidation of common institutional frameworks at the supranational level is presenting local levels of government with policies, practices and funding originating in Brussels. In these respects British local government is being drawn into a common net with that of other European countries. This may imply not only common interests but also competition between regions, towns and local authorities to provide the conditions which attract new more freely moving investment, skills and citizens.

The changing European context has generated a greater interest in learning from each others' political and managerial practices. In central and eastern Europe this is a matter of urgency as new government systems are established. In western Europe there are opportunities to compare the responses of different structures and traditions of government to common issues: the redefinition of the state's role in economic development and welfare, calls for new forms and levels of political participation and control, assertions of localism, demands for more responsible and accessible service provision, efficiency in the face of fiscal constraint. This opportunity to learn has particular pertinence in the British case where after 25 years of periodic reform, local government is once again due to undergo radical transformation in its structure and procedures, and where the construction of a form of regional government is on the political agenda. On the other hand, the recent British experiments with marketization in public policy have some fascination in other countries facing criticisms of efficiency and effectiveness in the public service.

The differences can be exaggerated but British local government is distinct from continental European models on several dimensions. It has no constitutional status except what is based on understanding; as the 'creature of parliament' it is easily exposed to redefinitions of its authority, role and even existence. Its functions are defined by parliament on the *'ultra vires'* principle: the 'general competence' which applies in continental European countries may not mean that local government does more in practice but it legitimizes its status as a level of government addressing all community affairs.

Other European local systems may account for less (Greece, Portugal, Italy, Luxembourg) or more (Netherlands, Norway, Sweden, Denmark, Austria, Switzerland) of public expenditure, but they frequently have much wider responsibilities going beyond their spending functions. They have a variety of forms of direct political executive, unlike the British model which formally merges the legislative and executive roles. Their local levels have generally seen less or no agglomeration or boundary redrawing, leaving them in all cases smaller and probably more easily understood by citizens. But most continental countries also have intermediate levels of government which are larger than the English and Welsh counties and which have often retained many of the important public services (health, water, energy) which have been nationalized and privatized in Britain.

The last main comparison which we will make here is that central and local government appear peculiarly insulated from each other in Britain, both administratively and politically. Forms of collaboration, unified career structure, post-holding at different levels, representation of the local at the state or national level, and integrated party structures are among the instruments which appear to make for less conflictual relations elsewhere. Significantly, the review of local government initiated in the last year of the 1987–92 Conservative

Government was directed at change within local government rather than at the relationship between the centre and local levels.

A leading issue in that review was the question of the form of the political executive. This is not simply a matter of internal management but relates to the central question of the balance between command structures and local accountability. How do different executive systems (committees, cabinets, boards, mayors, city managers) affect the efficiency of administration and the effectiveness of democracy? How do they affect the role of political representatives?

In this volume John Stewart considers the principles on which the British collective executive, combined with the legislature, is based. He identifies the implications of alternative executive systems and reminds us that change can be brought about by building on (rather than scrapping) existing practices. The following four articles show how such an evolutionary approach has been adopted in countries whose executive systems have, at least partly, shared the British collective approach. Baldersheim analyses Oslo's experiments in shifting from an aldermanic to a cabinet system, changing not only the model of political organization but also its relationship with the administration. The executive may now further evolve into a ministerial model consolidating political over official control of the administration.

Montin's account of reforms in the relationship between politics and administration in Sweden describes a vigorous debate which will be familiar to readers in Britain and elsewhere. Since 1945 there have been the classical shifts from top-down managerialist reforms, to a concern with political participation and decentralization, to a new managerialism combined with an assertion of the merits of privatization and user control. What is distinct from Britain in the Swedish case is the extent to which the experiments in new forms of management and contracting are locally inspired rather than centrally imposed.

Grunow describes the movement in North Rhine-Westphalia from the 'British model' to a strong executive leadership; current reforms propose a new mayoral model. He identifies the implications for majority and minority parties, for officers and for the influence of external interests. This leads him to consider whether reform processes in East Germany are repeating mistakes by modelling themselves on reforms in West Germany rather than by building on their own practices.

Rolla describes the way in which the functioning of Italian local government has been affected by Act 142 of 1990, which has meant a major shift of power to the executive, consolidating and streamlining what had already been occurring informally in terms of the relationship between legislature and executive.

Lastly, we return to the British case and Crawford's analysis of the British central government's resistance to the signing of the European Charter of Local Self-Government. In particular he questions the Conservative Government's objection to local 'general competence' and greater financial freedom.

RICHARD BATLEY AND ADRIAN CAMPBELL
Institute of Local Government Studies
University of Birmingham

The Internal Management of Local Authorities in Britain – The Challenge of Experience in Other Countries

JOHN STEWART

THE CONSULTATION PAPER

The government in Britain has issued a consultation paper on The Internal Management of Local Authorities in England[1] as part of its review of local government. This paper follows previous consultation papers on the structure and finance of local authorities.[2]

This paper is a consultation paper in the full sense of the term. It recognizes that in some authorities the present system works satisfactorily 'and where this is the case the Government have no wish to impose changes' (para. 16). It suggests the need for experimental projects.

> For the longer term, the Government would decide in the light of the outcome of experiment, whether, and if so how, changes should be applied more widely to local authorities. But they do not wish to impose a single management style on local authorities; they see great merit in authorities' building on best practice and developing arrangements which suit their local circumstances [para 42].

The paper is intended to initiate 'a full and wide-ranging debate' (para. 40). That is to be welcomed.

It is too readily assumed that the form taken by local authorities in this country is the only possible form that can be taken by local government. Thus it has been assumed, almost without question, that local authorities will be controlled by an elected council

- with elections for separate constituencies within the authority;
- with all councillors elected in the same way and assumed to have equal authority;

- with normally between 30 and 100 councillors;
- with executive authority vested in the council;
- exercising its main functions through committees.

None of these characteristics of local authorities are necessary features of local government. Local government takes different forms in other countries and an interesting feature of the consultation paper is the use made of that experience to suggest alternative models. The appendix contains brief descriptions of models of executive management in France, Italy, Germany (Bavaria and Hesse), Ireland, Denmark, Sweden and the United States of America.

The consultation paper is an invitation to innovation and uses experience of other countries to reinforce innovation. Authorities have been prepared to innovate. Clackmanshire District Council[3] has followed the example of pre-reorganization Monmouth Borough Council in abolishing all committees with the council itself meeting to take all required decisions. Tower Hamlets and Rochdale have taken further than other authorities the development of area committees in place of the traditional service committees. Lincolnshire County Council has developed an advisory role for specialist members in relation to the trading units it is establishing for common services. A number of authorities (including Avon, Bexley and Clywd) are departing from the traditional committee way of working by distinguishing between settings for strategy or policy-making, for operational control or for reviewing performance. Such changes show the capacity for innovation present in local government.[4]

There are, however, certain features of local government that are laid down by legislation and which limit the capacity for organizational innovation in local government. The electoral arrangements are one example, but the main focus of the consultation paper and hence of this article is on 'executive management', which, it is argued, needs new models as opposed to the traditional committee system.

THE KEY PRINCIPLES OF THE TRADITIONAL COMMITTEE SYSTEM

Three key principles determine the organizational form of local authority in Britain:

1. the council is the political executive;
2. the council cannot delegate to individual councillors, but only to committees;

3. committees must reflect in their composition the political balance on the council.

These principles support the traditional operation of the committee system.

The Council is the Political Executive

The council is responsible for all that happens in the working of the authority. It makes policy and sets the budget and ensures that they are carried out. This obviously differs from the organization of government at national level, where a fundamental distinction is drawn between parliament as legislature and the cabinet as executive.

A similar distinction between the council as the representative body and the separate political executive is a feature of the system of local government in many countries – although more sharply drawn in some countries than others. The political executive can be collective, as in Italy, or individual, as in France. In these countries it is appointed by the council, but it can be separately elected, as in parts of Germany or the USA. The political executive, not the council, is responsible for the working of the authority. The role of the council is to set the budget and approve major policy, which in Latin countries and elsewhere is cast in legislative form described as ordinances of the council.

The principle that the council is itself the political executive and as such is in charge of the organization and management of the authority underlies the operation of the traditional committee system, since it is normally through committees that the council exercises its responsibilities. That principle legitimates and at times almost seems to require the committees' involvement in operational management.

The Council Cannot Delegate to Individual Councillors

A council cannot delegate responsibilities to individual councillors even if they are chairs of committees. It can only delegate to committees (which in turn can only delegate to sub-committees) or to officers. Any doubt on this point was removed by the *Hillingdon* case in 1986.[5]

Chairs have no formal authority in their own right. They gain their authority in practice from their ability – except in a hung situation – to command a majority on the committee, but their position depends upon the committee. Individual councillors have no formal decision-making powers. This restriction on delegation supports the operation of the committee system, since it rules out the possibility of individual positions of councillor authority.

Committees Must Reflect in Their Composition the Political Balance on the Council

This provision was introduced by the Local Government and Housing Act of 1989. It bars the appointment of a majority party committee exercising effective political leadership. In practice, there is likely to be a leadership group on most councils holding key positions in the party group and on the council, but that group cannot be given official recognition in the working of the authority. Prior to the legislation, a number of authorities recognized the existence of such a leadership group through the creation of one-party policy committees, although often on an advisory basis.[6] Political reality was to be recognized in the working of the authority.

The result of the legislation has been to re-reinforce the role of the committee as a setting for formal decision-making as opposed to actual decision-making, which takes place in unofficial settings such as group meetings or meetings of chairs called by the leader of the majority party. The legislation in effect hid the political reality of policy-making.

The Impact of These Principles

These principles support the operation of the traditional committee system. In particular they support – although they do not necessarily require – the concern of the committee with the day to day working of the authority.

These principles also limit the development of alternative modes of working that would:

- recognize the existence of a leadership group;
- create individual positions of authority for councillors;
- reflect the reality of political control.

They limit therefore alternatives to the traditional committee system.

The Traditional System

The traditional committee system has a number of features, some but not all of which derive from the principles set out above:

- the committees are based on the main services of the authority or on its central functions;
- they meet on a regular cycle of meetings;
- each meeting deals with the routines of current business as well as with policy issues;

- they operate with agendas, often of more than ten items and in some instances up to 40 or more;
- they meet in public, except for specific items which can be considered in private session;
- they have the formal setting necessary for authoritative decision-making;
- they are attended by officers as advisers to the committee.

The traditional committee system has been criticized as involving the councillor in unnecessary detail, as focusing councillors on particular services and on the operational management of the service, and as being an inadequate setting for policy discussion or for the review of performance.[7] The consultation paper highlights 'the time-consuming and cumbersome nature' of committees, which it implies, although without any systematic examination of the issue, deters 'able and experienced councillors' from standing for election (para. 23).

While attention has focused on the weaknesses of the traditional committee system, it also has its strengths. The committee system involves all councillors – front benchers and back benchers, majority and opposition, in the work of the authority, giving them access to information and an involvement in decisions that many MPs would envy, which, as the consultation paper recognizes, would be restricted in some of the models it proposes (para. 38).

Any system has its strengths and weaknesses well shown in the contrast between councils and the House of Commons. Whereas reformers in local government may seek to reduce the role of committees, those in parliament seek to extend them. In local government the complaint is that councillors are too much involved in the work of the authority, while in parliament the complaint is that the ordinary member has little influence on the work of government. The challenge is to retain the strengths of the local government system while overcoming its weaknesses.

Broadly there is a choice between approaches based on reforming the traditional committee system and approaches which alter fundamentally the nature of the working of the local authority by abandoning the principles that support that committee system. The consultation paper opts for the latter, focusing on replacing the committee system by a separate executive.

THE SEPARATE EXECUTIVE

In the British local government system the council is the executive as well as in effect the 'legislature'. The issue is whether there should be a separate executive. The council would approve major policies and set the budget but the executive would then be responsible for running the authority as well as submitting major policy proposals and formulating the budget for the council.

The advantages claimed for the separate executive are that it enhances the effectiveness of the authority by giving clear direction to the authority and that it aids accountability by showing to the public where responsibility for the actions of the authority lies. It avoids the absorption of a general body of councillors in the detailed working of the authority, avoiding 'the time consuming and cumbersome nature of the committee system'. It does not necessarily mean the disappearance of committees as such, but would mean that they would not normally be executive committees concerned with the operation of services, but rather advisory committees concerned with policy formulation or with reviewing performance.

A Political Executive

A separate executive can be a political executive or an officer executive, although the emphasis of the consultation paper is on the former. There are two key choices about the form of the political executive.

1. Should it be appointed by the council or should it be separately elected?

The argument for separate elections, particularly when associated, as it normally is, with the proposal for the election of an individual (although the consultation paper also considered the possibility of electing a collective executive) is that it focuses responsibility and accountability. The problems lie in the relationship between the executive and the council if they are separately elected. There is no guarantee that the executive, if elected separately from the council will have a majority in the council.

The operation of the separately elected executive will depend on the way political parties organize themselves, including how the candidates for the executive are selected.

There is a clear difference between whether the candidates selected are first and foremost politicians (as can be the case in the United States[8]) or whether they are in effect professionals with an identified political allegiance (as can be the case in Bavaria, where lawyers are normally chosen[9]), although one would surmise that the former would be the more likely in practice.

Appointment by the council avoids most of the dangers of conflict between the council and the executive. It would fit more easily with the workings of political parties and groups. Indeed the danger might be that insufficient consideration would be given to the need for change in their working.

2. Should the political executive be an individual or should it be a collective?

The argument for an individual political executive, whether elected as in Bavaria or in parts of America or appointed as in France (a model strangely left out of these proposals in the consultation paper although set out in the Appendix) is that it gives clear direction to the council and again that it focuses responsibility and accountability. The individual holding that position gains prominence locally and can even gain prominence nationally, particularly when, as in France, the role can be combined with a position in national politics. One danger that is often seen in such a proposal is that it can lead to too great a concentration of power.

The collective executive is the more familiar model in the British political system and developments in local government might be based as suggested in the consultation paper on a cabinet model. Examples of a collective executive are found in Europe, for example, in the junta in Italy: 'The Junta is the municipality's executive body: it has certain independent powers; it may be authorized by the council to act on its behalf and, in emergencies, it can act in the council's stead.'[10]

We have then four possible models for the political executive:

(i) a separately elected individual political executive (commonly called the elected mayor);
(ii) a separately elected collective political executive (a theoretical possibility, but probably not a practical runner, although discussed in the consultation paper);
(iii) an individual political executive (commonly called the appointed mayor) appointed by the council and representative of the majority of that council, except of course in hung authorities, where the executive may not command a majority;
(iv) a collective political executive (which can be described as a local government cabinet system) appointed by the council, and representative of the majority of the council, except of course in hung authorities, where minority administrations are possible.

The degree of independence of the executive varies. There are countries in which a political executive is associated with the continued existence of service committees. This is the established pattern in Scandinavia where there is (apart from experiments with the cabinet system) an executive board composed of representatives of all parties. Thus the executive board in Denmark is described as holding 'a very central position in local government ... In fact the municipal executive board has the last word in all matters to do with money, planning, personnel and municipal administration, before the final decision is taken by the council as a whole'.[11] The existence of service committees with executive responsibilities alongside the executive board means that those Scandinavian models occupy an intermediate position between the traditional British system and the separate political executive, although in some British authorities the Policy and Resources Committee has developed a similar role.

The Officer Executive

An officer executive could be a collective executive, but is more likely to be an individual on the model of the city manager in America or a county manager in Ireland. The officer executive can be appointed by the council, as in America, or by some external agency or staff commission, as in Ireland. It could in theory be elected, but we assume that such a proposal would turn the officer executive into a political executive.

Historically, the officer executive has developed as a reaction against political corruption, but the advantages claimed for it today are usually on the grounds of efficiency and organizational effectiveness. The officer executive is clearly in charge of the organization and responsible for making decisions far beyond the present responsibilities of a chief executive in Britain. It can be argued that such a proposal gives effective professional and management direction to the working of the authority.

Against the proposal it can be argued that it takes too much power away from the elected council and ignores the reality that many decisions that have to be made in the working of a local authority are not decisions merely governed by considerations of efficiency and organizational effectiveness, but value choices that should be determined politically whether by council and committee, as is traditional in this country, or by a political executive, as discussed above.

SCRUTINY OF THE EXECUTIVE

The consultation paper recognizes that the concentration of power through the creation of a separate executive raises the issue of safeguards against the abuse of power. The paper discusses the development of scrutiny committees based on parliamentary select committees. Some may doubt whether such committees have sufficient powers to provide effective scrutiny.

Certainly the issue of scrutiny has to be faced. It is interesting that when Oslo introduced the cabinet system described elsewhere in this issue,[12] the role of committees in scrutinizing the cabinet's proposals was emphasized, all proposals requiring council approval being reviewed by committees whose recommendations are then considered by the council. These committees can also investigate specific issues. The combination of roles gives these committees a stronger potential for scrutiny than select committees in the British Parliament.

The actual operation of any arrangements for scrutiny will, however, depend on the balance of parties on a council and the way political groups operate. It will in particular depend on the extent to which the party group (or groups) that support the executive or allow a degree of freedom to members of scrutiny committees to develop that role and that would require significant changes in the degrees of control exercised by party groups over individual councillors. It is, however, an issue that has to be discussed if the need for scrutiny of the powerful executives being considered is to be met.

REFORMING THE COMMITTEE SYSTEM

All the proposals remove from the council its executive responsibility, eliminating thereby the need for the committee system as we know it. If, however, it is considered that there are strengths as well as weaknesses in the traditional committee system, other alternatives that involve reform of that system merit consideration, although only one such model is proposed in the consultation paper because of its emphasis on the model of the separate executive.

Building up the Leadership Role

There is in most local authorities an accepted political leadership, constituted by the majority group, recognized as such by the officers and consulted by them on that basis. The emphasis may be on the leader of the majority party or on the leadership group. The leadership has no formal position in the council beyond the positions they happen to hold. A few councils give formal recognition to the position of leader of the council, but it is not, of course, possible to delegate responsibilities to that position.

The danger is that the formal institutions of decision-making give no recognition to the actual processes of decision-making. This confuses the working of the authority presenting dilemmas for officers because their formal responsibility to the council may conflict with their responsibility to the majority party and its leadership. It prevents the development of clear political responsibility, because the effective party settings for decision making remain outside the main structure of the authority.

The political leadership could be given recognition in the working of the authority without creating a separate political executive. Such an approach was developing in authorities through the creation of one-party policy committees, but was stifled by the provisions of the Local Government and Housing Act on the composition of committees. Such constraints could be removed and the development of recognition for the leadership role could be encouraged. A leadership group could be given recognition without necessarily being a separate political executive. It need not eliminate the service committee, but would create a powerful policy committee because it would be composed of the political leadership. The absence of any opposition councillors would make it more likely to be the setting for actual as opposed to formal decision-making.

The consultation paper proposes one model which would permit these developments. It proposes reconsidering the need for minority representation on all committees although with safeguards for their right to raise issues on the council. The creation of a powerful executive, but alongside other committees, resembles the established pattern in Scandinavian countries described above, where, however (apart from experiments with the cabinet system), the executive board is composed of representatives of all parties.

Other Changes in the Traditional Committee System

The consultation paper focuses on the need for a political (or in one case an officer) executive. It does not give much consideration to other changes in the internal structure of local government. It does not, for example consider decentralization in local authorities, even though that has been an important development in Europe, particularly in Italy and Sweden.[13]

Too often it is assumed that the form taken by the traditional committee system is the only possible form that could be taken by a committee system. Clearly that is not the case.

Four broad areas of change are considered.

(a) The structure of committees

It is assumed that committees should centre on the operation of the main services provided by the authority and upon its central functions.

Yet some local authorities have shown that there are other possibilities. Area committees can focus not on particular services but on particular geographical areas and be concerned with all that happens within them.

As set out earlier in the paper some authorities separate committees for policy-making from those for decisions on day to day management (or indeed from performance review).

(b) The nature of the cycle

The frequency of meeting reflected in, for example, the monthly cycle of meetings found in many authorities underlies the criticism in the consultation paper of the committee system as cumbersome and time consuming. However the real issue may not be the length of the cycle, but the assumptions that underlie it. The undifferentiated cycle dominates the working of the authority. The agenda of one meeting is no different from any other. It can consist of up to 40 items in which short-term matters of operational concern jostle with longer term issues. A differentiated cycle would distinguish the purpose of meetings. While a number of meetings could be reserved for more routine business, specific meetings could be designated for setting the committee's strategy, for reviewing organizational effectiveness, or for performance review as well as reserving meetings for in-depth discussion of major policy issues.

(c) The conduct and business of meetings

The introduction of a differentiated cycle opens up the possibility of different forms of meeting which could be developed even within the undifferentiated cycle. The formal setting of the committee necessary for authoritative decision-making can inhibit the discussion desirable for policy exploration. There is a need for settings to discuss policy or to review performance freed from the constraints of the formal setting.

(d) The possibility of roles for individual councillors

Councillors gain their roles from committees, of which they are chairs or members. A few authorities have experimented with giving councillors specialist roles to develop interests in and give advice on particular topics or to take an interest in a particular activity. The council and the committee cannot however, delegate authority to an individual even if he or she is chair of a committee, and the consultation paper puts forward one model which eliminates that restriction. The restriction on delegation re-enforces the dominance of the committee system and inhibits the exploration of alternatives based on individual responsibilities.

CONCLUSION

There is a remarkable uniformity in the political structure of councils, although that structure is only to a certain extent determined by legislation. There are, however, indications of a readiness by local authorities to innovate and experiment, although that is limited perhaps as much by assumptions about the necessity of the traditional committee system as by the requirements of legislation.

There are a range of possible alternative developments. Those fall into two broad categories.

1. The development of a separate executive

    A. Political executive
    (i) a separately elected individual executive
    (ii) a separately elected collective executive
    (iii) an appointed individual executive
    (iv) an appointed collective executive

    B. An officer executive.

2. Reform of the present structure which can involve different aspects

    A. a development of the leadership role;
    B. changes in the committee system;
    C. the development of individual roles.

The consultation paper focuses on the first group of changes. It is hoped that local authorities will consider a wider range of alternatives. It would in any event be unwise, as the consultation paper recognizes, to prescribe one approach for all authorities. Circumstances vary. But, perhaps equally important, we have little understanding of how various proposals will work in the British political system and political culture. Each will probably prove to have its own strengths and weaknesses.

What is required is to release the capacity for innovation that lies within local authorities. This involves the removal of legislative constraints on, for example, one-party committees and delegation to committee chairs, but more is required to challenge constraints on ways of thinking, although the symbolic effect of the change would itself be a stimulus to new thinking.

The consultation paper suggests that 'A range of new approaches should be implemented in a few authorities so that they can be fully evaluated on an experimental basis' (para.40). A commitment to pilot projects and experiment is to be welcomed as a challenge to traditional assumptions; it is hoped that they are not limited to the models put forward in the consultation paper and that innovation is not limited to those experiments. Legislative change need not wait for the results of the pilot projects, if that legislative change is desirable in its own right and as a symbol of the commitment to change

NOTES

1. Department of the Environment, 1991.
2. 'The Structure of Local Government in England'; 'Local Government Finance' (Department of the Environment, 1991).
3. Ken Ennals and John O'Brien, *The Enabling Role of Local Authorities* (Public Finance Foundation, 1990).
4. Michael Clarke and John Stewart, *The General Management of Local Government* (Longman, 1990).
5. Widdicombe Report on The Conduct of Local Authority Business (HMSO, 1986).
6. Widdicombe Report on The Political Organisation of Local Authorities, Research Vol. 1 (HMSO, 1986), pp. 111–13.
7. See *We Can't Go On Meeting Like This* (The Audit Commission, 1990); John Stewart, 'The Role of Councillors in the Management of an Authority' in *Local Government Studies*, Vol. 16, No. 4 (1990).
8. Gerry Stoker and Hal Wolman, *An Elected Mayor for Local Government* (LGMB, 1991).
9. Alan Norton, *Notes on Local and Regional Government in Advanced Western Democracies* (Federal Republic of Germany, 1987).
10. *Management Structures in Local Government* (Council of Europe, 1986), p. 16.
11. *Local Government in the Nordic Countries* (Kommuneforlget, 1991), p. 40.
12. Harald Baldersheim, 'Aldermen into Ministers', p. 18 below.
13. Paul Hoggett, 'Political parties, community action and the reform of local government in Europe' in Paul Hoggett and Robin Hambleton, *Decentralisation and Democracy* (School of Advanced Urban Studies, 1987); L.J. Sharpe (ed.), *Decentralist Trends in Western Europe* (Sage, 1979).

'Aldermen into Ministers':
Oslo's Experiment with a City Cabinet

HARALD BALDERSHEIM

WILL THE EXECUTIVE FUNCTION BE THE FOCUS OF LOCAL GOVERNMENT REORGANIZATION IN THE 1990S?

Discussions on the proper organization of the executive function in local government are now taking place in many Western countries. The growth of local bureaucracy caused by new functions and the expansion of old ones since the 1960s have made political control over municipal administration an increasingly exasperating task for local politicians. Traditional models of democratic control seem to be under strain in many ways. In the 1970s more grass-roots participation was the fashionable solution for improving the workings of local democracy. Perhaps new forms of executive organization will be the solution of the 1990s?

The existing forms of executive organization are many and varied. In order to put the changes in Oslo's executive in a wider perspective, perhaps at the risk of oversimplification, I shall maintain that most executives may be placed on a continuum ranging from those that are predominantly political to those that are predominantly administrative, with a range in between. The American 'strong mayor' may be the best-known example of the political type, with the directly elected mayor exercising both political and administrative control and co-ordination.[1] The German 'Oberbürgermeister' has much the same position and function in the local government systems of southern Germany.[2] Copenhagen's and Stockholm's plurality system with elected mayors for the various administrative branches on a proportionate basis would also belong clearly to the political type, although the plurality and proportionate principles mean that this executive is less integrated than the 'strong mayor' one, and therefore perhaps less 'strong'.

The predominantly administrative type of executive would include again an American example as perhaps the best known – 'the city manager'. The city manager also has a German counterpart, 'der Stadtdirektor'.[3] In municipalities with figures like these, executive control and coordination is primarily the responsibility of an appointed figure who works for the council on contract, often for a stipulated term, and who is granted much leeway by the political masters in day-to-day operations. The political leaders are expected to play a more aloof role in municipalities of this type. The fact that they do not always act in such a restrained way is a source of friction in quite a few municipalities. The rest of Denmark outside Copenhagen also falls into this category, and so do Norway and Great Britain, although the Danish managers have to share somewhat more power with their leaders than their Norwegian and British counterparts.[4]

The interesting thing about Oslo's experiment is not only that it meant a change from an administrative to a political type of executive, but also that the change meant such a dramatic swing from one extreme to another. It is not easy to find precise counterparts to the 'parliamentary' model introduced by Oslo in 1986. The nearest thing may be the Italian system, where the council elects a '*giunta*' on a majority basis. The *giunta* is politically responsible to the council for how it performs the executive function and may also be ousted by the council during an election period.[5]

Discussions on the advantages and disadvantages of the various executive models seem not to have reached definitive conclusions. The positions in the American discussion of the pros and cons of the 'strong mayor' versus the 'city manager' forms of the executive have been that the former are more responsive to popular and political pressure (but also more open to political abuses, its denigrators claim) while the latter is a foundation for responsible and restrictive financial policies (and an embodiment of middle-class views and values, according to its opponents).[6] The political executive will be more spending oriented, while the administrative one will be more inclined to hold back on spending and taxes.[7] The original body of research on the subject claimed to be able to confirm the existence of these relationships while later contributions have concluded that there is no evidence that certain types of executive are associated with certain types of financial policies.[8]

Some German states are now also contemplating a change of executive mode. North Rhine-Westphalia is planning a switch from a city manager model to an 'Oberbürgermeister' or strong mayor system.[9] There, the arguments in favour of a change are that this will enhance popular control since it will be clearer to the electorate who has responsibility.[10]

What happened in the case of Oslo? How did the new model work out? What happened to financial control? The latter question is especially interesting since Oslo introduced this reform in the midst of a financial crisis – indeed, as a solution to the crisis – which may seem a rather odd choice considering the traditional view of the strengths and weaknesses of a strong political executive.

However, before we turn to a discussion of the outcome of the Oslo experiment, a more detailed presentation of the new executive model is needed.

THE CITY OF OSLO'S 'CABINET EXECUTIVE' AND RELATED REFORMS

The City of Oslo has, since February 1986, been going through an experiment with a new city charter, which allocates power in a completely new way among the actors in the city government. This experiment with a 'city cabinet' is the most radical break with established organizational patterns of local government in Norway that any local authority has undertaken so far. The new charter is an attempt to organize local politics according to 'parliamentary' principles which take the national form of government as a model. The experiment breaks with two traditions in local government organization in Norway: the alderman model of political organization and the directorate model of administrative organization.

The alderman model (*'formannskapsmodellen'*) assumes local politics to be a matter for laymen sharing a responsibility for community affairs. Local problems can be solved through friendly discussions between neighbours. The model allocates positions of influence between the political parties on a proportional basis, that is, according to party strength in the local council. These posititions of influence allocated are seats on the board of the council and seats on a local authority's numerous standing committees. Proportional representation is supposed to favour the development of a political climate of consensus, cooperation, and reasonableness. In the case of Oslo, what came to be increasingly seen as a problem with this type of decision-making style was that the lines of responsibility and accountability tended to be blurred, so that under conditions of increasing financial austerity, parties and individuals were tempted to behave irresponsibly. In the corridors of Oslo's City Hall it was said, half-jokingly, that the city council was in the habit of passing budgets with the volume of expenditures favoured by the Social Democrats and the level of taxation favoured by the Conservatives. Also, the control of administrative agencies was thought to suffer from a lack of overall coordination and a lack of clear political guidelines.

The central premise of the directorate model ('*rådmannsstyre*') is that administration is a task for and should be conducted by professionals highly trained and specialized in their respective fields. The directorate model draws a sharp distinction between administration and politics. All administrative appointments should be strictly meritocratic and non-partisan. All matters to be considered by the council and other political bodies are prepared and presented to them by the director or, as in Oslo, the directors. The directors have tenure, and can only be fired if misconduct can be proven. Even then, they have a right of appeal to the Ministry of Local Government. The directors, therefore, have a strong influence over the agenda of the political bodies, and over the range of alternatives they are invited to consider.

Faced with a severe financial crisis, an accumulated deficit of nearly one billion kroner, a decision was made to change the city charter. A new charter, it was hoped, would result in better and more responsible government. The city charter was launched as a means to promote six different goals:

1. improve political control over the administration;
2. clarify the lines of political responsibility and accountability;
3. greater emphasis on 'the view of the whole' in decision-making;
4. more adaptability in service provision;
5. more scope for employee participation;
6. better service for the public.

These goals were to be achieved through two structural changes: (1) introducing a 'city cabinet', elected on a *majority* basis by the council, and with a 'parliamentary' type of accountability to the council, and (2) giving the city cabinet the right to *instruct* the administration.[11] What happened, basically, was that the city cabinet took over the powers and functions formerly possessed by the eight directors, whose positions were abolished. The parliamentary relationship to the council meant that the city cabinet had to be backed by a *majority* constellation in the council. It had to resign if a vote of no confidence was passed, or if it asked for a vote of confidence and failed to get it.

The two structural changes were supplemented by reorganization at the top and intermediate levels of administration. The gist of these reorganizations was to replace the directorate model of administration with a *managerial* one. Under the directorate model there was no clearly defined head of administration, the directors were equals under the authority of the council (with the financial director, perhaps, as a *primus inter pares*). They were each supposed to provide the council with independent professional advice and to carry out the council's decisions as they thought fit. The foundation of good administration was assumed to be professional competence in specialized fields. The managerial thinking, introduced along with the new city charter, emphasized administration as a skill in its own right, and maintained that this general sort of skill should guide the professionals. Accordingly, a position for a general manager was created, to whom the administrative branches under the leadership of the various professionals were to be clearly subordinated. I shall call him the city manager in the following. To emphasize his superior position, the city charter expressly made him the exclusive link of communication between the political and administrative sides of the city government. The cabinet members were to channel all their communications and directives through him, and the subordinate departments were also to reach the cabinet and other political bodies solely through the manager. The arrangement was also meant to emphasize the city cabinet as the locus of *political* responsibility. In Oslo, this was a revolutionary arrangement since, previously, the existence of the eight directors with their separate chains of command, and the numerous standing committees, had meant that communication and interaction between politicians and administrators were frequent and widespread. The advantage was a rapid dissemination of information throughout the organization, but at the price of fragmented chains of command and responsibility.[12]

At the lower levels of administration, in the service departments, efficiency gains were hoped to be achieved by moving more decision-taking further down the hierarchy. Wider powers were delegated to the service departments, especially concerning reorganization, personnel matters, and reallocation of funds up to a certain amount.

When all the new schemes are put together, it can be seen that they represent answers to two different types of problem. One problem was the increasing party-politicization of local government. In Norway, party politics in local government is a post-war phenomenon in many places, and it increased especially in the wake of the amalgamations of the 1960s.[13] When party-politicization becomes intense, as in the case of Oslo, it exerts a strain on the alderman form of government, which in its origins is non-partisan, although it has, over the years, accommodated a moderate level of party conflict. However, in the daily affairs of most local authorities, party political distinctions still do not matter much. Oslo, however, was not only already highly politicized, but financial difficulties and the prospect of service cutbacks contributed to making local politics increasingly adversarial. Politics was no longer only a question of taking credit for new services but also a question of shouldering the blame for cutbacks. In such a climate, a parliamentary form of local government seemed a better embodiment of the political processes.

The other problem addressed by the Oslo reform was that of the growth of the service machinery and the higher standards of service provision expected by the public. Oslo employed around 50,000 people (including part-time workers) and had become a vast conglomerate of operations. At the same time, dissatisfaction with public services was growing and media reporting on some services was highly critical. The new political leadership in the city cabinet clearly felt that a more businesslike approach to local service provision was called for, and that much could be learnt from industrial corporations and business firms. However, at this stage, better management rather than privatization was hoped to provide the solutions to improved service provision.

So, Oslo's reforms reflect both a concern with the city as an increasingly politicized arena, and also with the requirements of increasingly complex processes of service production. The city cabinet was the answer to the first problem, the city manager was part of the answer to the second. Could these two solutions co-exist, or did they pull in such different directions with regard to leadership styles and approaches to the roles that frictions were bound to occur? How did the experiment work out in practice? To what extent were the expectations, as expressed in the list of goals above, fulfilled?

To answer these questions, I shall draw on material from an evaluation study which the city initiated, and which was carried out during the first two years of the experiment (from February 1986 to July 1988).[14] The evaluation study was structured around the six goals the city sought to achieve. Here, I shall concentrate mostly on the first three goals, those that dealt most directly with the city's political processes, but some material concerning the other aspects of the reform will also be presented.

IMPROVING POLITICAL CONTROL OVER THE ADMINISTRATION

The process of decision-making and also the political agenda used to be structured by the division of work between the city's administrative branches (health, education, transport, and so on). Problems, plans, and financial requirements of the administrative or service-providing agencies created a steady and heavy stream of issues that were channelled into the political arena for solutions, decisions, or just as information about what was going on. Politicians often felt overwhelmed by this stream and found little room or time for their own initiatives or visions. In order to cope with the workload of information and issues, many tried to become 'super-bureaucrats'. This seemed to have been the fate especially of many of the full-time salaried politicians that several cities, including Oslo, introduced in the 1970s. However, having left the role model represented by the layman amateur councillor, they have had difficulties developing distinctive alternative roles for politicians.

Did the new city charter change this state of affairs? Was political control intensified? Was the city cabinet able to make its presence felt in the administration in ways different from the political bodies of the previous regime?

Our main impression in this respect was that the political agenda was still largely structured in the same way that it was before: the administrative agencies *acted* and the city cabinet *reacted*. The stream of issues from below was and is so heavy that it was not humanly possible for a few politicians faced with an army of bureaucrats to change that situation fundamentally. However, we also observed that the city cabinet began to behave more strategically towards the administration. The administrative bodies were increasingly asked to produce strategic plans for their areas. The cabinet tended to specify more and more carefully the issues it wanted considered in these plans. If a draft plan was thought to be unsatisfactory from the cabinet's point of view, it would be returned to the department in question to be reworked. This back-and-forth process might be repeated several times over. The cabinet would only present the plan for discussion in the council after it reflected the cabinet's political views and priorities satisfactorily.

When asked by us, the various administrative agencies said they felt that political guidelines for their work were laid down more clearly now than before. But they also felt that the political guidelines were of a more partisan nature than before. Furthermore, all documents presented to the council and to the wider public were now presented as the city cabinet's documents and views, whereas, before, plans, reports, and so on were presented in the name of the director whose agency had produced it in the first place. And if the views of the administration were different from those of the political masters, that would be evident in the documents that finally reached the council. Now, only the cabinet's opinions and preferences would be known. Before, an administrative agency would also be able to receive the credit for new initiatives and become known for its high professional standard and creative solutions. After the reform, credit would go to, or was supposed to go to the cabinet. This change was intentional, of course, and was supposed to be balanced by blame-taking for failures and misdeeds. However, some agencies said they felt less motivated to do their best now that someone else was taking the credit. They clearly felt alienated by the idea that they as professionals should not be allowed to shine among other professionals. While this probably represented a remnant of the directorate model, expressed as ideas about the proper role of professionals in city government, it had not yet, at the time of the evaluation study, been tackled by the cabinet in a constructive fashion. These were the professionals that the politicians would have to work through whether there was a city cabinet or an aldermanic board, but at this stage the relationship was strained.

LOCAL PARLIAMENTARIANISM – A CLARIFICATION OF POLITICAL RESPONSIBILITY?

How does a parliamentary political system work at the local level? Did clearly identifiable factions of insiders and outsiders emerge in a city council that consisted of seven different parties? Was it possible to keep a faction together for long enough so that it could make a serious attempt at majority government? Were the instruments of parliamentary democracy – votes of confidence and no confidence, for example – employed, and to what effect?

The first set of questions, whether factions of insiders and outsiders emerged, and how important these lines of divisions were, was studied by analyses of city council documents and votes. Our chief hypotheses were that (a) on the assumption that structural changes do matter, party constellations of insiders and outsiders would in fact emerge, (b) the overall level of conflict would increase, and the largest number of conflicts would be those between the most important parties in the insiders and outsiders factions respectively, and (c) since the propositions now placed on the council's agenda were of a more partisan nature than before, more counter-propositions would be produced by the other parties in the council.

The Pattern of Insiders and Outsiders

In the city council of 1986, the liberal or non-socialist parties had a majority of one over the socialist parties. Of four parties on the liberal side, the Conservatives were the largest single party; on the other side the Social Democrats dominated over two other smaller parties. After some rounds of negotiations on the liberal side, the Conservatives formed a city cabinet, but had to rely on the support of two other parties (the Progress Party on the far right, and the Christian People's Party more to the centre). This constellation survived several motions of 'no confidence' put forth by the socialist side in the city council. In one case, the majority for the cabinet was just one vote, which indicates that block voting for and against the cabinet took place. However, the number of block votes between the parties of the insiders and outsiders had actually declined, from eight in 1985 (the year before the new charter) to just five in 1987. After the local election in 1987, the Conservative cabinet was reinstated in office. The non-socialist majority had now increased to six council seats.

Did the new city cabinet also succeed in establishing itself as a focus of attention for public opinion, or was it all just a palace revolution in City Hall, unnoticed by the wider political environment? Newspapers soon grasped that a new locus of responsibility had emerged. They began to refer to proposals put before the council as 'the city cabinet's proposals', whereas they were previously presented in headlines as 'the director's proposals'. Interest groups increasingly tried to arrange to see members of the cabinet to present their case, while earlier they would send delegations to the city council's meetings (the practice of receiving delegations has not been discontinued by the council, however).

Opinions outside City Hall also seemed to become increasingly polarized, at least as presented by the media. The city cabinet's proposed budget cuts of June 1988 (see below) caused demonstrations to be held in the streets of Oslo by city employees as well as citizens. Some of the demonstrations ended in riots and confrontations with the police on a scale not seen since the Vietnam demonstrations in the 1960s.

The Pattern of Conflict

A growing overall level of conflict was expected. However, the proportion of uncontested or unanimous decisions had actually increased when the spring session of 1985 was compared to the spring session of 1987 (29 per cent against 31 per cent of uncontested decisions).

As mentioned above, the dominant parties among the insiders and outsiders were the Conservatives and the Social Democrats respectively. There was no tendency for these parties to oppose each other more vigorously than before. The proportion of joint voting, that is, voting for the same alternative, actually increased (81 per cent of all votes in 1985 and 83 per cent in 1987). The parties to the left of the Social Democrats were those that most often voted against the city cabinet.

Counter-policies

In this case, our expectations were confirmed. More counter-proposals or supplementary propositions were put forward by the political parties represented on the council. The increase was around 60 per cent. All the socialist parties were more active in producing counter-propositions than they had been before, while the non-socialists became less active. So it seemed that the opposition chose to express its dissident views through the suggestion of alternative policies and courses of action on a limited number of issues rather than through an indiscriminate 'nay-saying' to all cabinet proposals. This pattern may point to the existence of a highly responsible opposition as well as to the continued existence of the political climate associated with the aldermanic form of government.

BETTER COORDINATION – IS FINANCIAL MANAGEMENT THE TESTING GROUND?

The impetus for changing the city charter and introducing the city cabinet was the desperate state of the city finances in 1984/85. During 1986 and 1987 the financial position seemed to improve, partly because of higher revenues than expected, and partly because special measures to manage the burden of deficits had been negotiated with the Ministry of Local Government. However, in May 1988 it became publicly known that the city's finances were in trouble again. A deficit had built up during 1987 which, together with what remained of the former one, meant that the situation was even worse than it had been in 1984. Did this failure to balance the books indicate that coordination of the city government and 'the view of the whole' was no better now under the new city charter than it was before?

The question is not easy to answer since the set-back of the city economy was, to a large extent, clearly caused by occurrences outside the city cabinet's control, for example, reductions in city employee working hours negotiated at the national level, increased contributions to the national pensions fund imposed by the central government, growing urban problems requiring higher supplementary social benefits, and so on. Also, the other larger Norwegian cities, working under the old order, had run into even greater financial difficulties than Oslo. Bergen, for instance, had a deficit that corresponded to 17 per cent of its current budget, while the figure was only six per cent for Oslo. So, Oslo shared the fate of other cities. But its new city charter had *not* enabled it to do better than other cities, and not better than it did before in terms of financial management.

The level of responsibility reached under the new regime may be illustrated with a tale about the 1987 budget that resulted in so much overspending. The city cabinet's own presentation of the budget shows that they knew they would have problems in financing the level of activity they would like to maintain. When faced with the problem of balancing the budget, a city has three principal options: cutting expenditures, increasing revenues, or trying to bridge the gap through measures improving productivity and so being able to get more value for money. When faced with these choices, the cabinet said it intended to pursue the third strategy, bridging the gap through productivity measures. This amounted to giving the nod to the administrative departments to go ahead with their activity plans although the appropriations did not match the plans. The budget might still have been saved had the cabinet pressed on with systematic measures to improve efficiency and cut manpower, hard as that may be in labour-intensive local services. We were not able to identify such measures, but with this background, the ensuing deficit was not surprising, and it demonstrated clearly that fundamental problems remained to be tackled in the city of Oslo.[15]

MANAGERS AND MINISTERS – CAN THEY COEXIST?

As mentioned above, two changes in administrative organization were tacked on to the city cabinet reform: the introduction of the city manager with overall responsibility for coordination and communication with the political bodies, and delegation of authority to service departments in order to enhance their adaptability and flexibility in service provision.

The city manager's position was increasingly soured by complaints from the service departments over delays in their dealings with the city cabinet. They said they often had to wait too long for guidelines from the political bodies, and that the manager was acting as a bottle-neck. In reality, delays in the political responses to issues presented by the departments were often caused by the selective attention exercised by the cabinet. The members of the cabinet tended to give priority to issues *they* felt were politically important, sometimes to the neglect of the departments' concerns. This process of selective attention was, of course, not so visible to the departments, they only observed that the manager received their memoranda, and that thereafter they might not hear anything for months. The manager, for his part, was not in a position to disclose the deliberations of the city cabinet to the departments.

Gradually, pressure was building up to circumvent the city manager, both from above and below. Members of the city cabinet felt it to be increasingly cumbersome to have to go through the city manager every time they wanted some piece of information from a department, or if they wanted some investigation carried out. The cabinet members soon started to practise a division of work that largely corresponded to the city's administrative subdivisions, although they had authority and responsibility only as a collegial body, not as individual 'ministers'. The informal division of work at the cabinet level was soon perceived and acted upon by the outside world, which started to ascribe responsibility to individual members such as 'the cabinet member for health', 'the cabinet member for transport', and so on. Such a development also seemed to be appreciated by the service departments, who had complained that the new city charter had cut them off from contact with the political processes. In 1989, the cabinet applied to the Ministry of Local Government to be allowed to change the city charter so that cabinet members might be given individual authority over departments, that is, the introduction of a full-blown ministerial model. Such a change would clearly affect the position of the city manager, who felt that he would then become more of a financial adviser and less of a general manager and coordinator. The issue has not yet been decided by the Ministry.

CONCLUSIONS

The debates over the role of the cabinet members – collegial board of governors or full ministers – and the position of the city manager – general manager or financial adviser – clearly indicated difficulties of coexistence between the two organizational models of city government. The ministerial model on the one hand and the managerial one on the other hand are parts of wider institutional structures, parliamentary democracy and the market economy. These structures require certain role-sets to function consistently. If you want a parliamentary democracy with responsible and accountable ministers, you have to complement the high-profile political role of a minister with that of a neutral, faceless bureaucrat, confined to the role of an adviser. If you want your local authority to be run more like a business firm, you have to give the necessary powers to a manager, who can control the various executive branches of the city and who has the authority to knock them into shape if necessary. The complementary political roles will then have to be more distant exercises in goal setting and monitoring, perhaps also with scope to act as watchdog or ombudsman, but with little involvement in day-to-day affairs.

Oslo's experiment may have provided a lesson in the limits to institutional cross-breeding. However, we also registered positive change towards many of the goals Oslo set itself with the reform, so the experiment also provides an example of local capacity to change and adapt. In that respect, Oslo could well provide a model for the central government.

NOTES

1. E.C. Banfield and J.Q. Wilson, *City Politics* (New York: Vintage Books, 1963).
2. D.P. Conradt, *The German Polity*, (New York: Longman, 1989).
3. D. Schimanke (ed.), *Stadtdirektor oder Bürgermeister* (Basel: Birkhäuser Verlag, 1989).
4. E. Riiskjaer, *Kommunale forvaltningschefer* (Arhus:Forlaget Politica, 1982); J. Stewart, *Management in Local Government: A Viewpoint* (London: Charles Knight, 1971).
5. S. Cassese (ed.), *Annuario 1991 delle autonomie locali*, Vol. 1 (Roma: Edizioni delle autonomie, 1990).
6. E.C. Banfield and J.Q. Wilson, op.cit.
7. R.L. Lineberry and E.P. Fowler, 'Reformism and Public Policies in American Cities' in M. Bonjean et al. (eds.), *Community Politics* (New York: The Free Press, 1971).
8. T.N. Clark, 'Community Structure, Decision-Making, Budget Expenditures, and Urban Renewal in 51 American Communities' in C.M. Bonjean et al.(eds.), op.cit.
9. Innenministerium des Landes Nordrhein-Westfalen, *Reform der Kommunalverfassung in Nordrhein-Westfalen* (Dusseldorf: NRW, 1991).
10. G. Banner, 'Kommunalverfassungen und Selbstverwaltungsleistung' in D. Schimanke (ed.), op.cit.
11. Previously, only the city council and the board as *collegial* bodies could issue instructions to the directors and their agencies in the form of formal decisions.
12. H. Baldersheim, 'Administrative Leadership in a Big City' in G.M. Hellstern et al. (eds.), *Applied Urban Research. Proceedings of the European Meeting on Applied Urban Research*, Essen, 2–4 Oct. 1981 (Bonn: Bundesforschungsanstalt für Landeskunde und Raumordnung, 1982).
13. J. Sundberg, 'Participation in Local Government: A Source of Social Democratic Deradicalisation in Scandinavia?' in L. Karvonen and J. Sundberg (eds.), *Social Democracy in Transition. Northern, Southern and Eastern Europe* (Aldershot: Gower Publications, 1991).
14. H. Baldersheim and T. Strand, *'Byregjering' i Oslo kommune. Hovedrapport fra et evalueringsprosjekt*, Report July 1988. LOS-senteret, Bergen, 1988.
15. More consistent financial policies have been pursued, however, from the summer of 1988, combining cutbacks and productivity measures. But still the deficit (summer of 1991) stands at three billion NOK.

Recent Trends in the Relationship Between Politics and Administration in Local Government: The Case of Sweden

STIG MONTIN

INTRODUCTION

The aim of this article is to describe and to some extent analyse recent trends in reorganizing Swedish local government structure. The focus is on the relationship between the political and the executive structure in a wide sense. First, the development of local government reforms and changes during the post-war period are briefly described in three phases. Then, three particular issues relating to developments during the 1980s are examined. Finally, some distinctive aspects of this development are discussed.

THREE PHASES IN LOCAL GOVERNMENT DEVELOPMENT

Local government's development from the 1940s to the 1990s can be divided into three phases. The first phase – ranging from the late 1940s to the mid-1970s – was primarily orientated toward enhancing the policy efficiency of local government. Thus, the national government launched a series of reforms aiming to strengthen the local government bureaucracy and to ensure the provision of financial and other necessary resources. Following reforms the number of municipalities decreased from 2,498 in 1951 to 1,037 in 1952 and 280 in 1974. A few sub-divisions increased the number to 284 in 1989. By drastically reducing the number of municipalities, the new local governments came to enjoy a stronger tax base and hence greater economic and administrative resources. In 1946, the typical municipality would have about 3,000 inhabitants. The second major amalgamation programme implemented in the 1970s prescribed the ideal population size to be at least 8,000 inhabitants. This population base was considered necessary to launch an effective system for the provision of social welfare and a comprehensive school system.[1] The average population in the municipalities is now about 16,000 inhabitants (median value).

The first reform affected only rural municipalities, while the second was inspired by central place theory, introducing one unitary municipal concept instead of the three earlier ones; cities, boroughs, and rural municipalities. Taking the enormous increase in public responsibilities into account this development signifies a decentralization from central to local government. From the perspective of the individual citizen, however, the development was not so simple. In many respects it meant a centralization as distance to local government authorities increased.

The amalgamation reforms triggered a series of research projects and evaluations. The first major evaluation showed that after the 1960 reform local governments enjoyed greater financial and administrative resources. At the same time, however, the overall level of participation had declined. Thus, although enhancing local efficiency, the national government had to recognize the problem of decreasing participation and ultimately less political accountability and democracy.

The second major evaluation, conducted after an amalgamation programme in the 1970s, arrived at a different conclusion. The results indicated a general tendency towards increasing participation and better knowledge on political matters, coupled with increased party politicization and increased politico-administrative professionalization of local affairs. However, participation now took other forms and used other channels than before; people now seemed more inclined to approach bureaucrats and interest organizations rather than party constituency organizations and elected representatives when trying to influence local government politics. Since one of the indisputable consequences of the amalgamation was the reduced number of elected representatives, this change in political behaviour can probably in part be attributed to these reforms.[2]

In short, the evaluation portrayed local governments as democratically vigorous, politically dynamic, and administratively viable political bodies. Along with this glamorous picture, the evaluation also suggested that corporatist trends could be observed in local political decision-making and implementation. The overall argument was that the prevailing fear of decreasing local democracy – voiced by the many critics of the amalgamation reform – was exaggerated. As many politicians and researchers interpreted the results of the evaluation, local democracy in some respects seemed to be increasing, in other respects decreasing.

Already prior to the completion of the evaluation the second phase of local government development was embarked upon in the mid-1970s. This time the objective of the reform could be described as 'bringing democracy back in'. Several measures initiated and implemented during the late 1970s served this purpose, for example, local consultative referendums, sub-municipal councils with decision-making status and powers, as well as reforms and projects to support party constituency organizations and to encourage community members to engage in communal decision-making. The 1977 revised Local Government Act revolved around these and similar measures to stimulate participation and to relax central guidelines on municipal organizational structures and powers. However, after the election in 1982 when the social democrats came back to power after six years of non-socialist government, the central government announced a 'new public administration policy'. Decentralization, user-democracy, service-orientation, better leadership and freedom of choice were some of the keywords in this policy. At local level several municipalities had already started processes towards the 'renewal' of local government. This was the beginning of a third development phase.

The shift from the second to the third phase is marked in at least three ways. First of all there was a change in the 'reform culture'. The post-1945 period up until the early 1980s had witnessed a series of local government reorganizations in Sweden as a result of comprehensive, large-scale top-down reforms.[3] From this moment on local government reorganization reforms changed course, becoming more experimental, more 'learning by doing'. The ambition was to let the local government renewal start from the bottom, identifying problems at the local level. Among the experiments the 'free commune reform' was announced as the most radical and important one.[4] Nine, and then more than 30, municipalities and four counties were allowed to organize their activities and to use state grants with a higher degree of freedom. The experiment was intended to start a process of change at the local level and then was to be continuously evaluated. This was quite a new way of reorganizing the public sector.

Secondly, the decentralization became the trade-mark for nearly every change and experiment. By the beginning of the 1980s there was a changing attitude to decentralization within the Social Democratic Party (SAP). During the 1970s the social democratic government had rejected the demands of decentralization. In 1970 the SAP party leader and Prime Minister Tage Erlander wrote that 'When people demand "decentralisation", they do so without considering that centralisation within the public sector is a means to attain equality and security for the citizens'.[5] For several reasons the ideological course changed and now the overall policy is that 'the 1990s shall be the decade of the local level. The public sector must be handed back to the people'.[6]

However, the term 'decentralisation' is 'an almost "empty" term, a kind of camouflage behind which a diverse range (of often incompatible) political and organisational strategies can find cover'.[7] This is also the case of some of the renewal experiments at local level in Sweden. The label covers both political decentralization, such as sub-municipal councils, and minor administrative rationalization reforms. Often the term is used mainly in a symbolic manner, as an indicator that something positive is going on.

Thirdly, triggered by the fiscal crisis of the nation-state there was a radical change in defining the crucial problems to be attacked by the state. Thus, 'effectiveness' and 'efficiency' were now regarded as more important policy objectives than 'democracy'. Local actors became less interested in how to increase citizen participation in general and more interested in finding new systems of management. As in other parts of public administration, ideas and models from the private sector were imported, usually based on an ideal image of how private enterprises should work and be organized.[8]

KEY ISSUES

Among the several issues related to this development and particularly touching upon the relationship between the political and the executive structure, three topics will be discussed: political control and accountability, effectiveness/efficiency and citizen participation problems.

Political Control and Accountability

Defined as an institution with viable representative democracy, local self-government is based on the possibility of enhancing and improving political control and responsibility.[9] According to the principle of representative democracy there is a demarcation between political and administrative functions. A fundamental principle of Swedish local administration is that it is supervised by directly elected representatives, that is, the council of the local authority. The task of the executive committee is to supervise the administration of municipal affairs and to keep itself informed about the activities of other municipal committees. It is the highest executive body of local government and as such responsible for the economic affairs of the municipality and for long-term planning.

Before the recent change in legislation, which will be discussed below, special legislation required each municipality to have special committees for particular tasks, for example, an education committee, an environmental and health protection committee, a social committee, and a building committee. They are to be responsible for day-to-day activities in their special areas, prepare items for the council, implement decisions and make certain decisions of their own in accordance with laws and municipal regulations.

One of the conclusions from the second evaluation of the reorganization of local government was that the local government structure had changed 'from administration by laymen to administration by professionals', which, among other things, led to the consequence that 'The administrators in all communes have now assumed not only responsibility for implementation but also an important role in the process of policy formulation from the politicians'.[10] Although the local administration became professionalized and bureaucratized, there was still participation from the elected politicians within administrative issues:

> 'Local government in Sweden is distinguished by the fact that the elected representatives participate directly in the handling of a matter at all levels, from drafting to decision-making and implementation, which means that their tasks include those which in the national administration are the sole concern of salaried officials.[11]

These quite contradictory conclusions highlight the relations between political control and responsibility on one hand, and administrative autonomy on the other. This problem has been a focus of discussion and several reforms have been initiated to enhance political control.[12]

In the beginning of the 1980s a system of 'government by objectives' was introduced. The aim was that the elected politicians should be more concerned with formulating and stating goals according to people's needs and with systematically evaluating the outcome of the service. However, research findings and the debate have indicated several problems related to this new system. The goals are often vague and give the administrators great space for different actions. Objectives are often formulated by a few politicians together with only some leading administrators, which leads to a risk of marginalizing lay-politicians. If measurable objectives are developed, they are often narrow and quantitative. Finally, instruments and measures for evaluation are poorly developed. Some findings indicate that 'government by objectives' leads to decreased political control and accountability because of the vast room for discretion given to the administrators.

In several municipalities a new structure of formal relationships between political and executive structures has been introduced and established. This is known as 'ordering and performing organizations'. The idea is that – as an extension from 'government by objectives' – political activities should be separated from producing activities. The performing organization should be less day-to-day controlled by committees and freer to handle financial and other resources. This means that the political bodies are moving back from the administrative structure. This is a change in problem definition compared to the discussion during the late 1970s. Then the problem was how to enable the decision-makers to control the administration. The ideology behind this new organization policy is better to adjust service production to environmental demands, more free from political control. Service production is viewed as a less 'political' matter than before, consisting of 'neutral' economic activities which should be less restricted by rules and short-time decisions.

One of the elements in the 'free commune reform' was that the municipalities became free to choose their own committee structures. Not only the selected 'free communes' but several other municipalities demanded the right to adjust their committee structures. As a result of this change in the municipalities, the new Local Government Act – passed by parliament in June 1991 – gave all municipalities (and county councils) the right to decide their own structure of boards and committees. This means that the system of compulsory committees will disappear from 1992. The main effect of this deregulation is a reduced number of committees and, as a consequence, a reduced number of elected representatives.

Another trend during the 1980s has been to decentralize, and to some extent privatize, the responsibility for service production. It started in some municipalities by nominating parts of the administrative structure as 'result units'. These units handle financial and other resources more freely than before and are supposed to compete with one another and, in some cases, with external entrepreneurs. Beside this the number of private entrepreneurs, co-operatives and companies with mixed ownership has increased during the last ten years. In several municipalities the 'performing organization' is moving towards a public/private mix. The debate about 'privatization' has gradually changed from being an ideological issue to a question of practical ways

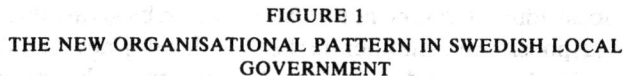

FIGURE 1
THE NEW ORGANISATIONAL PATTERN IN SWEDISH LOCAL GOVERNMENT

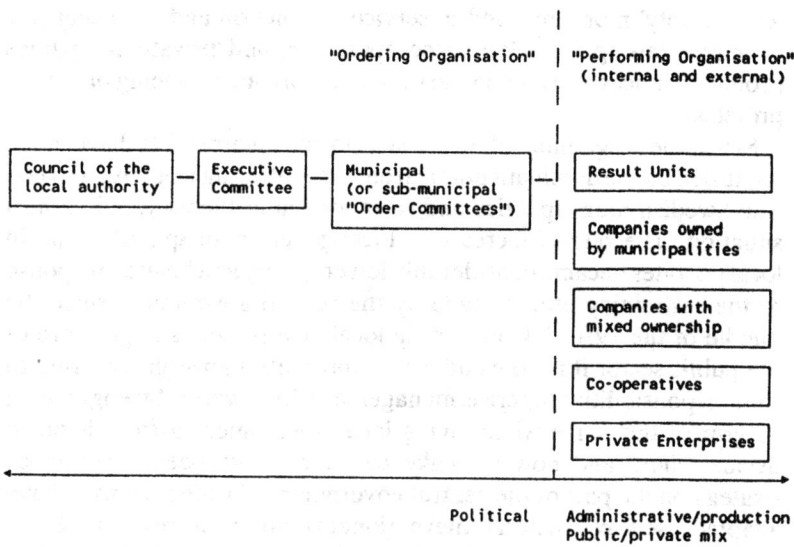

of organizing service production. Sometimes the labels 'alternative associations' and 'alternative responsibility' are used to depoliticize the debate. The new organization pattern in the municipalities is illustrated in Figure 1.

Effectiveness and Efficiency

As with many other terms, 'effectiveness' and 'efficiency' are used in a multiconceptual way to refer to different things. Sometimes they refer to the fulfilment of qualitative goals and people's needs, sometimes they refer to ways of reducing public expense. The debate on local government renewal has changed its focus from the former to the latter. Since the mid-1980s, there has been a striking predominance of the management-biased output aspects and an obvious disregard for things like input or outcome in non-monetary terms. In a quantitative content analysis of reorganization documents, covering the late 1980s, in 121 Swedish municipalities, we found an overwhelming stress on 'harder' management and cost-oriented values, while 'softer' values like citizen needs, political party activity, legal rights and product quality were totally ignored by more than half of the municipalities.[13]

Several projects and experiments have been initiated. One has been to make local administrators more cost-conscious by giving them more resource responsibility. Another has been to develop new quantitative criteria for local resource distribution. A third strategy has been to get 'civil society' more involved in service production and financing (for example, raising fees, letting co-operatives and private companies produce services and mixing the public and private financing of certain projects).

Since the beginning of the 1980s local governments have been identified by the dominant political elites as suffering from fiscal stress. The Swedish municipalities and counties found themselves in a new situation. The rate of increase in local government spending and in local tax rates became considerably lower, partly as a belated response to the restraining efforts made by the central government since the middle of the 1970s.[14] Considering local government's large share of the public sector it is no wonder that the central government tried to shift responsibilities for crisis management downwards. Strengthening its grip of the purse while giving local government a freer hand to decide where and how to make cuts may have been a conscious strategy on the part of the central government. Sweden seems to have adapted itself to a general international trend in this respect.[15] Since 1990 the pressure on local councils to reduce costs has increased as they are not allowed to raise their taxes for the years 1991 and 1992.

Projects and reforms with the objective of increasing efficiency dominate the municipal picture at the beginning of the 1990s and they are often contradictory to more democracy-oriented experiments. In the rhetoric such conflict is not mentioned, but often the question is raised whether local government can 'afford' local democracy.

Citizen Participation

The concept 'citizen participation' is vague and may stand for several different activities and relations.[16] It can mean participating as an elected representative in decision-making bodies, like local committees and boards, in local party groups or interest groups, in the actual provision and performance of services and in contacting politicians and administrators in an effort to exert influence on local decision-making. Traditionally, a difference is drawn between participation through representative democracy (party participation and contacting elected representatives) on the one hand, and participation outside the representative bodies (demonstrations and interest group activities) on the other. However, both forms of participation refer to the input side of the political system, to use David Easton's framework. User participation in service performance, on the other hand, refers to the output side of the system (implementation).

For at least two decades the parties have been suffering from legitimation problems, such as low recruitment of new members and activists, particularly young people and women and a reduced capacity to mobilize and activate the population. According to several research results, participation in local branches of established parties and contacting local representatives are declining activities. This does not mean that political interest among Swedes has declined, it means that they use other channels than the traditional parties. In the late 1970s this was defined as a problem of local democracy and reforms aiming to enhance party legitimacy were introduced.

A 'sub-municipal reform' was introduced to increase citizen participation and to vitalize the party organizations. By 1991, 23 local government authorities had divided their territories into sub-units governed by sub-municipal or sub-county councils. These councils were not given the responsibility for *all* functions delivered by local government. They were granted authority for one or several policy areas, mainly the 'soft' sectors such as culture, leisure, primary education and social services. The sub-municipal reform may be seen as an effort to restore something of the local political culture from the pre-amalgamation period with smaller territorial areas. The aim was most of all to recover the local party organizations. It may also be viewed as an effort to modify a strongly sectorized, functional organization through the introduction of a geographical dimension. Finally, it may be looked upon as a device used to increase local government's responsibility for reducing public expenditure growth. The three interpretations do not, of course, exclude each other.[17]

Presented in the early 1980s, this sub-municipal reform was believed to be a very important instrument for enlivening local democracy. However, the expectations and hopes of a reduction in bureaucracy, quicker decisions, and shorter time from policy initiative to implementation have not been fulfilled.[18] Furthermore, only slightly improved citizen participation and a small increase in party activity can be demonstrated.[19]

When evaluations suggested that the reform did not raise the expected level of participation, the advocates of the reform redefined its purpose, now emphasizing the efficiency aspects of the councils.[20] The declining interest in the reform is expressed by the fact that out of 50 municipalities which in the middle of the 1980 were investigating the prerequisite for a sub-municipal reform, 40 desired to abstain from it. Thus, today among policy-makers and national bureaucrats, the reform is categorized as one geared to enhancing bureaucratic and service production efficiency, not to increasing democratic participation.

In the public sector in general, and at local level in particular, citizens began to be viewed as 'users' and 'customers'. One of the elements in the new policy of public administration is 'user democracy'. The idea is that 'users', like parents, should participate in and exert influence on service production. All municipalities, especially the 'free communes' are expected to develop this user democracy. According to the new Local Government Act, committees are allowed to delegate decision-making to subordinate actors with the condition that they consult user groups.

A great number of projects have started in the municipalities. Some of them have been more successful than others. However, research results indicate several difficulties in developing user democracy. Some of the problems are about defining the users, the difference between participation and influence, the conflicts between user participation and representative democracy, conflicts between user interests and professional interests, conflicts within the 'user collective', and how to find practical arrangements for user participation.

Besides this user perspective there is a growing customer perspective. Here the stress is put on the 'freedom of choice'. The idea is that, for instance, patients should have the right to choose between health centres and parents to choose between schools for their children. The main difference between these two policies can be conceptualized in terms of 'exit' and 'voice'.[21] While freedom of choice is a matter of possibilities to 'vote with the feet', user democracy is a matter of possibilities of exerting influence on goals and performance in a given institution.

Freedom of choice as a policy has grown and has often been put above the policy of user democracy. At the beginning of the 1980s the social democratic government defined user democracy as an alternative to privatization, but by the 1990s privatization had become more a practical issue than an ideological one.

The stress on user participation and freedom of choice has implications for the relationship between the political and the administrative (performing) structure. The stress is put more on the performing side of the system than on the political side. There is now in Sweden a widespread conception among local government actors that the current problems they handle have nothing to do with democracy and citizen participatiogcoonceived in traditional terms. The focus is laid on how to emhancegfreedomeof choice for the consumers and users of public services and how to make production more efficient. There are differences between social democrats and non-socialist party elites, but during the last five years the social democratic government has become more concerned about freedom of choice, competition within the public sector, and contracting out than about solidarity and bureaucratic rules.

At the local level, the reducing number of political representatives are now, more than before, supposed to play the role of political managers over the administration, to formulate goals, follow up the implementation of decisions, and evaluate service production. Local politicians might well put more energy into this aspect of council's function than they do into traditional political functions, such as stimulating, mobilizing and supporting political participation among citizens.

CONCLUSION

So far the reorganization of Swedish local government has been described as if there were no political or ideological conflicts surrounding it. This is not the case. Even though the policy change is often presented in a depoliticized, neutral manner, there have been and still are ideological tensions between and within the parties. From the debate it is possible to pick up at least four positions.[22]

The position taken by the 'privatization advocates', mainly the Moderate Party and the Liberal Party, is an ideological standpoint of 'rolling back the state' and replacing public service organizations with competing private companies. They also argue for more individual responsibility in financing public services. This group would prefer a depoliticization of local government, meaning that the politicians should withdraw their engagement in the production of 'services' rightly belonging to the family.

The three other positions are more or less tied to the Social Democratic Party. The second group may be called 'traditionalists' because they criticize the new trends in local government from a traditional point of view. The argument is that government by objectives, ordering-performing organization structures, privatization, mix of private/public control and ownership, and the customer-oriented reforms jeopardize the system of representative democracy. They see a great threat to democratic political control and accountability.

The third group may be called 'decentralists' or 'popular movement advocate'. During the late 1970s and the beginning of the 1980s this group argued for better co-operation between local Government and popular movements, co-operatives and other local mobilizing groups. They also argued for decentralization as a means to democratize the municipal structure. Although this position has been weaker during recent years, there are still within the party advocates of user democracy and local political control instead of privatization.

However, at the beginning of the 1990s a fourth group, the 'economizers', seems to be the strongest. They argue that bringing a halt to public sector expansion ought to be the top priority in the foreseeable future. For them decentralization is first of all a question of making public services more efficient in economic terms. Privatization is an acceptable and even desirable form of decentralization since it should bring competition, and some efficiency, to public service production.

There will probably not be a large-scale privatization of local government service production and financing during the 1990s. However, the trend towards seeing the production of public services in the municipalities as politically neutral economic activities will probably grow stronger. This means that we will see several types of arrangement with a mix of public and private financing and production control. It is an open question what role the parties and the elected politicians will play in this new system.

NOTES

1. L. Strömberg and J. Westerstahl, *The New Swedish Communes: A Summary of Local Government Research* (Stockholm: Liber, 1984).
2. Ibid.
3. F. Kjellberg, 'Local Government and the Welfare State: Reorganization in Scandinavia' in B. Dente and F. Kjellberg (eds.), *The Dynamics of Institutional Change: Local Government Reorganisation in Western Democracies* (London: Sage, 1988), pp. 39–69.
4. Mellbourn, *Bortom det starka samhället* [Beyond the Strong Society], (Stockholm: Carlssons, 1986).
5. Cited in D. Söderlind and O. Petersson, *Svensk Förvaltningspolitik* [Administration Policy in Sweden] (Uppsala:Diskurs, 1988), p. 119.
6. Minister of Civil Service, Bengt K.A. Johansson, 1990.
7. P. Hoggett, 'A Farewell to Mass Production? Decentralisation as an Emergent Private and Public Sector Paradigm' in P. Hoggett and R. Hambleton (eds.), *Decentralisation and Democracy* (Bristol: SAUS, 1988), p. 215.
8. C.f. J.P. Olson, *The Modernization of Public Administration in the Nordic Countries. Some Research Questions. The Study of Power and Democracy in Sweden*, Report no. 19 (Uppsala, 1988).
9. A. Gustafsson, *Local Government in Sweden* (Stockholm: The Swedish Institute, 1983), p. 61.
10. L. Strömberg and J. Westerstahl. op.cit., p. 61.
11. A. Gustafsson, op.cit., p. 64.
12. P.O. Norell, 'Communal Administrators. The Swedish Case', paper presented at

the ECRP Joint Session of Workshops, Ruhr-Universität Bochum, 2–7 April 1990, Local and Regional Bureaucracies in European States.
13. E. Amna, *Reorganization and Value Allocation. Political Implications of Decentralization* (Örebro: Centre of Public Administration, University of Örebro, 1990).
14. B.-C. Ysander and T. Nordstrom 'Local authorities, economic stability and the efficiency of fiscal policy', E.M. Gramlich and B.-C. Ysander (eds.), *Control of local government* (Stockholm: The Industrial Institute for Economic and Social Research, 1985), pp. 347–398.
15. I. Elander and S. Montin, 'Decentralisation and Control: Central – Local Government Relations in Sweden', *Policy and Politics*, Vol.18, No. 3 (1990), pp. 165–80; R. Premfors, 'Coping with Budget Deficits in Sweden', *Scandinavian Political Studies*, Vol.7, No. 4 (1984), pp. 261–84.
16. S. Langton (ed.), *Citizen Participation in America* (Massachusetts: Lexington Books, 1978).
17. I. Elander and S. Montin, op.cit.
18. K. Kolam, 'Neighbourhood Councils in the Nordic Countries', *Local Government Studies*, Vol.17, No. 3 (1991) pp. 13–26.
19. S. Montin, 'Fran demokrati till management. Decentralisering inom kommunerna' [From democracy to management. Decentralization within the municipalities], *Staatsuctenshaptig Tidskrift*, 2, 1989.
20. Ibid.
21. A.O. Hirschman, *Exit, Voice, and Loyalty: Responses to Decline in Firms, Organizations, and States* (Cambridge: Harvard University Press, 1970)
22. R. Premfors, 'The "Swedish Model" and Public Sector Reform', *West European Politics*, Vol.14, No. 3 (1991), pp. 83–95.

Constitutional Reform of Local Government in Germany: The Case of North Rhine–Westphalia (NRW)

DIETER GRUNOW

INTRODUCTION: CONSTITUTIONAL ARRANGEMENTS OF LOCAL GOVERNMENT IN GERMANY

A constitutional reform for local government is currently being prepared in North Rhine-Westphalia (NRW). This situation offers an interesting background for the review of trends in the development of local government, because it bundles up different interests, concepts and goals in a very explicit way. The specific conditions of the ongoing debate can only be fully appreciated if the context – in terms of the overall structure of the political-administrative system (PAS) – is considered.

The first important contextual element is the anchorage of the existence and role of local government in the German constitution (Grundgesetz). In Article 28 the right of local communes or municipalities is stated to 'regulate all local affairs on the basis of existing law in their own responsibility' (Selbstverwaltung). An important consequence of this anchorage is a limitation of constitutional reforms in the more specific forms of communal constitutions (Gemeindeverfassung; Gemeindeordnung). Arguments about political desirability, economic advantages, and so on can be restricted by considerations about the compatibility with the Grundgesetz and the overall federal structuring of the German PAS. Consequently, the interpretations and decisions of the Bundesverfassungs-Gericht play an important role in the debate about the reform of the communal constitution.

Another consequence of the overall constitutional arrangement is the allocation of responsibility to the German states (Bundesländer) for the formulation of communal constitutions. As a consequence of long-term traditions in the rights and structures of commune and town governments as well as of the specific influences of the Allied forces after the Second World War, different models of local government (defined by communal constitutions) can be found. Thus, a description of the structure of German local government always has been a differentiated table of various components. Although this does not cover the whole spectrum of possible alternatives, the comparison between these realised variations in the context of the German Grundgesetz plays an important role in all discussion about a change or overall reform of the communal constitution. This is also an important point of departure for empirical research – in addition to normative (legal) expertise. The recent debate in NRW has to be placed in the following more specific situation.[1]

- The existing model of local government is unique in Germany (although there are similarities with Lower-Saxony); it originated from the British model of local government with the (honorary) mayor and the (professional) town clerk or chief executive (in 1946). Another important feature is the fact that only the council members (Ratsmitglieder) are elected (for five years) by the citizens – all other functions and positions (including the position of the mayor) are allocated by the council.[2]
- The commune constitution in NRW has undergone quite a few – but rather partial – changes: 1948; 1952 (the first time by an autonomous state parliament of NRW after the Second World War); 1964; 1969; 1974; 1978; 1979; and 1984. In spite of much criticism concerning the 'model in use', the various reforms did not change the basic structure of the commune constitution. This has not been so in the recent debate where a more general alternative is taken into consideration: the model from Bavaria and Baden-Württemberg, the 'Südeutsche Ratsverfassung'. Consequently a much broader evaluation of the commune constitution is taking place, with many more arguments and more interests at stake.
- The picture of the German communes/municipalities has been influenced heavily by the regional and functional reform which was completed (basically) in 1978. Here also the different states pursued various strategies. For NRW the question of size and administrative efficiency has been dominant. The result was an extreme reduction of the number of communes (1967: 2,297; 1979: 373). In NRW the average commune has many more inhabitants than in the rest of Germany – which leads also to large administrative bodies on the local level. In this context, the second dimension of the reform,

democratic representation and participation,[3] seemed to be of less concern and consideration.
- A new element in the reform debate in NRW is introduced by the process of unification of East and West Germany. The development of 'administrative aid' from the west for the east includes 'vicarious competition' between different states of East Germany – which have their specific supporters in different states of West Germany. The competition is related to all political and administrative arrangements, which are decided upon within each state (including the formulation of the commune constitution). The 'partner' of NRW is Brandenburg. It is difficult now to 'sell' specific 'models' of local government in Brandenburg, when they are under reform in NRW. In addition, there are strong interests in East Germany to include more participation and decision rights for the citizens in the commune constitution. This is related to the experiences of the 'peaceful revolution' as well as to the persistence of a GDR law about local government ('Selbstverwaltung der Gemeinden und Landkreise in der DDR'), which was ratified by the last GDR parliament (Volkskammer) in May 1990.

ISSUES AND AIMS WITHIN THE REFORM DEBATE

The long-term territorial reform has made very explicit that the notions of democratic legitimation and political participation as well as administrative competence and efficiency are the main points of reference for the 'modelling' of local government (under the rule of the Grundgesetz). It has become clear that both goals are only partially compatible. In such a dilemma (or even multilemma) situation a circular variation of critical elements of the commune constitution is the expected reaction. The many partial revisions of the 'Gemeindeordnung' in NRW (since 1946) can be interpreted as a repeated rebalancing of different (not completely compatible) elements of the basic model ('Direktorialverfassung'). Thus it is guaranteed that only a small minority will 'lose' (influence, resources, domain of control, and so on) through this change. By reviewing the different steps of change since 1946 the important features ('variables') of the model can be identified. These features should also be of central concern for the more general reform under debate now.[4]

Issues Concerning Democratic Representation and Political Participation

The important elements of the design of local government are presented systematically (not as a historical process). The sequence does not imply a rank order.

(a) Election

It is defined by the Grundgesetz, that an elected body (council) should represent the interests of the citizens and should be responsible for the formation of local affairs. It is open, however, whether specific outstanding positions (like the mayor) should be directly elected by the citizens (or by the council members). In NRW the mayor is elected by the council, the choice thus depending on the majority party in the council.

(b) Functions and party-politicization of the council

To what degree does the council represent the citizenry? The council members are honorary politicians. This implies selective chances to different citizen groups to take over such a role. In Germany this has led quite often to an overrepresentation of public sector staff and private business-owners in the communal councils. And beyond that question, can the 'representatives' ensure the implementation of priorities of the 'represented' (or at least of themselves as 'locals') in the development of the commune/municipality? How strong is the dividing line between political parties and how much is it influenced by party politics on the national and state level (vertical guidance)? A development toward such a 'party-centred parliamentarism' has been observed and criticized during the last decade. The points of criticism are the increasing polarization within the council as well as the adoption of themes from 'grand politics' (on state, national, or international level) – an instructive example being the 'declaration of communes as nuclear-free zones' in the eighties. This has also constitutional implications: the guaranteed right of self-administration. This formulation in the Grundgesetz is interpreted as a limitation to 'grand politics' which has close connections with legislation on national and state level. In this interpretation the local level should not install any kind of competing government, but rather concentrate on qualified and reliable administration. This can, of course, include the consideration of specific local conditions and demands.

(c) Decision power and control

An important aspect of the role of the elected council is its position *vis-à-vis* the local administration. The NRW model is described as 'double-peak' (Doppelspitze – represented by the mayor and the head of administration) or recently as 'triple-peak' (now including the leader of the majority party). Therefore the question is discussed, whether the council has too little or too much power of decision and control over the administration. The autonomy and dependency of local administration has been a major issue for reforms of the local constitution: the council in NRW communes has the right to retract specific administrative tasks for review and decision; the council does not only elect the head of administration but also can dismiss him/her (with a two-thirds majority) during his/her appointment (normally eight years). This formal power leads to the question of competence of the decision-makers: does their knowledge and experience 'justify' an interference in administrative activities – especially if it concerns the local implementation of national or state law?

(d) Additional forms of citizen participation.

Besides the right to elect the council members and/or to be elected as council members, some other ways of 'including' the citizenry in local government have been established: sufficient information for the public about all important developments and plans (section 6b); the right of citizens to intervene in local affairs (by written propositions or complaints – section 6c); the role of (not publicly elected) competent citizens in the council and the boards (sachkundiger Bürger); the public character of council meetings (section 22.2). Additional more formal interventions of citizens into the decision-making process (Bürgerbegehren, Bürgerentscheid) are topics of the recent reform debate.

Issues Concerning Administrative Competence and Efficiency

The preceding arguments already indicate the interdependence between issues of political representation and independent professional administration. Both components of the commune constitution cannot be 'maximized' at the same time. The debate in NRW centres on the following topics:

(a) One-peak leadership

The fusion of the functions of mayor and head of administration is seen as one way to make the work of the council and of the administration less frictional. This should also reduce the dominance conflicts between the two roles. The main argument being that the area of autonomous political initiative of the council has steadily declined during the last decade. Laws with extended prescription for implementation, as well as the dependency on funds from the state and national levels, support this argument. One major consequence is the demand for administrative competence in local political leadership. Administration has to be law-based, efficient and responsive to the citizens – a difficult balance for the local administrator. Are the (honorary) representatives of the citizenry able to fulfill their guiding and controlling functions? One answer has been to strengthen the division of labour in the council by the establishment of numerous boards – which allow more accumulation of experience and competence in specific fields for a smaller number of council members. As a consequence most decisions are pre-arranged in the boards – in which members of the administration often play a dominant role.

(b) A more independent status for local administration

The role of administration can also be strengthened by the definition of 'current administrative tasks' which are defined as the rather autonomous domain of the head of administration and his/her staff. Another point of variation is the procedure of selection and dismissal of high-ranking administrators: how much influence comes from the council members (especially concerning the party affiliation of candidates) and how much influence is given to the administration (to secure maximum available quality and competence through the selection process)?

(c) Professionalization of the council members

Another option for increasing efficiency is to keep the extensive rights of the council but to reduce the number of its members and to increase its professionalization (that is, full-time occupation). A model under discussion stems from Lower-Saxony, which has basically the same local constitution as in NRW, but which has introduced a powerful administrative board (Verwaltungsausschuss). This board prepares all important decisions in co-operation with the administration.

The Diversity of Practical (Empirical) Experiences

To organize local government in the context of the Grundgesetz is a complex task which is related to multiple and in part competitive goals (performance criteria). The quality of local government depends not only on the basic arrangements of commune constitutions. The regional location, the size of the commune/city, the economy, the citizenry, the qualifications of the available political actors and administrative staff members are just a few of the additional influencing factors. Therefore, the commune constitution opens options for very different practical approaches to implementation by local politics and local administration (in NRW). It is nearly impossible to evaluate the overall performance of local government as a consequence of a specific constitution.

The 'history of small-scale reforms' in NRW emphasizes this conclusion. Many initiatives for change stem from the experience of a single case or very few cases – which is often not shared by others: an inadequate selection of the head of administration might lead to the demand for an easier procedure of dismissal; the interpersonal conflicts in the 'triple peak leadership' might lead to the demand for a fusion of leadership functions; the planning problems and respective conflicts might lead to a demand for more formal participation of the citizens, and so on. But in almost all cases one will find contradictory cases, which strengthen the arguments of those who want to keep the existing structure. And, in addition, there are almost always winners and losers in a process of change. This leads to different evaluations even within a specific (positive or negative) case. Evaluations depend on the position of the evaluator in the local PAS. Thus, it is easy to explain why there has not been a general change of the model of commune constitution in NRW until now (by the way, this is also true for all other German 'Länder'). It is also easy to see that such a reform is not tied to the interests of any one political party, in which the different functionaries are acting.

Starting from this 'definition of the situation', it must be asked why the Minister of the Interior (NRW), who is responsible for the preparation of the reform, chose the distribution of a questionnaire to some 18,000 council members, 1,200 heads of administration and their direct subordinates (Dezernenten), including special questions to some 400 mayors and 1,400 party leaders in the council. It is self-evident that this can only reproduce different experiences or different domain-related interests (for a strong council or a strong administration; for a strong representation system or for a strengthening of direct citizen participation; for a model of party competition or for a democratic consensus, and so on).

The results of the survey,[5] in which some 11,000 functionaries participated (with about 60 per cent response rate), meet these expectations precisely. One set of questions is concerned with the 'realities' *vis-à-vis* the constitutional prescriptions. For example, one question is concerned with the division of labour between mayor and head of administration: 'does the practice fulfill the norm?' The answer 'precisely' is given by 55.5 per cent of the mayors; by 45.5 per cent of the council members; by 44.9 per cent of the party leaders in the council; by 30.6 per cent of the heads of administration and by 21.4 per cent (!) of their direct subordinates (Beigeordnete). The opposite answer ('not at all') varies between 6.9 and 14 per cent; the others see partial 'deviations'. This spectrum of reactions is very typical for this type of question. It shows not only the expected variety of experiences and points of view, but also the difficulty of defining reform goals: are they focusing on bad practice or on inadequate norms and will the propositions improve the norms or the practice or both?

Another type of question asks for opinions about performance, quality, and deficiencies. Again just one example should be cited: 'does the right of the council to dismiss the head of administration (at any time with 2/3 of the votes in the council) make him too much dependent on the council (and especially the majority party)?' The answers show the following distribution: council members – 16.9 per cent yes, 74.3 per cent no; party leaders in the council – 14.9 per cent yes, 80.3 per cent no; mayors – 19.6 per cent yes, 75.4 per cent no; heads of administration – 66.7 per cent yes, 30.0 per cent no; their direct subordinates (Beigeordnete) – 49.6 per cent yes, 45.3 per cent no (the difference from 100 per cent indicates the proportion who did not give an answer to this question). This pattern of responses is repeated even for questions which do not relate to the division of labour, and suchlike, between the political and administrative roles. Thus, if they are asked whether the mayor lacks responsibility to represent the interests of the citizens, 51.4 per cent of the mayors and only 17.5 per cent of the heads of administration answer 'yes'.

The document, which has been produced on the basis of this survey, is a demonstration of the diverse interests and domains which are at stake if a general change of the commune constitution in NRW is attempted. (It should be mentioned, though, that this is to a large degree also the consequence of 'selected' or 'biased' questions; the questionnaire could have been constructed in a way that gives a more precise evaluation of different local practices.) The existing documentation, however, leads to the prognosis that the reform under discussion will not take place – if no other ('external') forces for change come into play.

EXTERNAL FACTORS WHICH INFLUENCE THE REFORM DEBATE AND CHANGE PROCESS

Although there is no especially pressing external factor which enforces a reform, many different influences may be observed. Only a very few will be mentioned here: those which in our view have the strongest impact on the debate.

Comparison and Competition Between Comprehensive Models

The unique situation in Germany with the different commune constitutions in the states gives the chance for a comparison between comprehensive models. This certainly introduces more interesting insights than any before – after comparison of partial changes. And, in fact, many practical and scientific contributions to the debate centre around the overall performance of different models. Of central concern in NRW is a comparison with the 'Süddeutsche Ratsverfassung' in Bavaria and especially in Baden-Württemberg. Two elements are important for this (South German) model: the mayor is elected directly by the citizens (for eight years); the major has the function of a chairman of the council (and of the representative of the council to the public) as well as the role of the head of administration (one-peak leadership). The dominating proposition is that this model is better coordinated and more efficient than the NRW model. As a side-argument the responsiveness of the directly elected mayor is mentioned. The general notion of this alternative under discussion is summarized in the term 'executive leadership, which is "accompanied" by the council'.[6] In contrast, the NRW model is named 'council as centre of legislative and programmatic guidance'.[7] One feature rarely included in the evaluation is this: in Baden-Württemberg citizen appeal (Bürgerantrag) and citizen decision (Bürgerentscheid) is also part of the commune constitution. It was established as a countervailing mechanism *vis-à-vis* the powerful position of the mayor. This component of the model is not 'advertised' in most of the propositions.

A more systematic review of the comparisons shows the expected selectivity of criteria applied.[8] As in most complex configurations advantages and disadvantages can be identified – depending on the evaluation standards. One of the most prominent protagonists of the Baden-Württemberg model, Banner,[9] uses three criteria for a comparison: budgeting, personnel policy, and citizen-policy (Bürgerpolitik). He emphasizes that his favourite model offers better performance in all three dimensions. But a close scrutiny of his evidence reveals only one non-normative evaluation criteria – the balance of the budget, which he finds to be attained more often in Baden-Württemberg. The other 'criteria' just repeat the formal elements of the model (like elections, staff selection, and so on). But even this more restricted thesis lacks evidence as Kunz-Zapf and Schramm[10] demonstrate in a comparative empirical analysis of 87 communes (with different constitutions). In sum, Banner is primarily interested in the efficient and correct management of commune/city tasks, which – as he rightly emphasizes – are to a large extent defined elsewhere (state or national parliaments and executive institutions). But the available evidence regarding the relative advantage of the Baden-Württemberg model is still not very compelling.

If one accepts the concentration on an efficient management there are still differentiations to be made, as Nassmacher[11] points out, concerning primarily the size and location of the commune/city, economic structure, long-term majorities in the council, and the question whether one deals with new problems and tasks or with traditional routine work. It is quite plausible that, for example, the ability of the council to balance the budget depends on such factors. Another perspective is brought in by Wehling,[12] a close observer of the Baden-Württemberg model. He emphasizes the participatory elements which – at least in a long-term perspective – allow the development of a specific political culture. This cannot be easily 'transported' into another context (that is, NRW).

This all indicates that a comparison of complex models does not reveal clear evidence about better or worse performance, which could induce the choice of another comprehensive model. In order to reach stricter performance statements a pre-selection of central issues (like efficiency) is necessary, as well as a specification of additional characteristics (like large cities with difficult economic transformation processes, and so on). The dichotomies used in the debate are not convincing enough to be used as goals and guidelines for the reform. Therefore quite a few authors suggest (again only) partial changes (but!) on the basis of a sound evaluation of the existing practice (not model!) as the most promising reform strategy (Thränhardt[13]).

Developments in the New East German States

The situation in the new East German states (Brandenburg, Saxony, and so on) is quite different from the situation in NRW, because a completely new commune constitution has to be established. The 'conserving' forces are much weaker than in NRW. The decisions that must be taken could be a much more thoughtful and weighted selection of a specific model from West Germany, a 'new mixture' of West German elements or even a completely new model (as long as it is covered by the Grundgesetz). Thus, this situation could lead to a more open and impartial review and evaluation of the existing alternatives.

But there are restrictions to such a strategy. An important one is the still effective DDR law on self-administration in East Germany (from 17 May 1990). It was a necessary step to enable the elected persons from the first democratic local elections (6 May 1990) to build up new structures and start work. The law adopts the basic premises of the Grundgesetz, and it puts much emphasis on citizens' rights of participation (Sections 16–18) – a consequence of the experiences of the 'peaceful revolution'. Concerning the elements discussed above, a 'new combination' is chosen: the functions of mayor and head of administration are combined ('one-peak model'), but there is no direct election of the mayor; moreover, the control functions of the council remain strong. Altogether, the notion of grassroots democracy is much more anchored here than in all models in West Germany.

This law is only of temporary importance, because since the states have been constituted the right to formulate the commune constitution rests with the new state parliaments (Section 100). It still has to be seen how much they rely on the principles formulated in this law. At the moment the first steps of a territorial reform for communes and districts is being prepared, which will also have consequences for the parameters mentioned above (number of inhabitants, size of the administration, division of labour with other public institutions, the economic situation, and suchlike). This at least opens up the chance of a well-thought out design of the commune constitution. It seems – so far at least – that the East German states are not willing to accept pressure from their West German colleagues. They might also stick to the participatory elements described above, because they still have to win the general acceptance of the population for democratic structures and procedures.

Influences, if not pressures, come from the many western 'advisers' acting in East Germany nowadays.[14] Some even describe this as 'colonization of East German administration' – especially on the state level, which had to be established completely from scratch. It is quite visible and also understandable, that most co-operating persons or agencies from the West try to 'sell' their model to their clientele: it is the thing that they know best or perhaps even the only thing they know of. The competition between West German states is in this way 'transported' into the East German states. In the case of NRW there is (by party affiliation) an especially close 'co-operation' with Brandenburg. Will this lead also to an adoption of the commune constitution in NRW, in spite of all critical debate? This question cannot be answered yet. With regard to territorial reform, it seems, at least, that NRW transports its 'big solution' to Brandenburg (few large districts and communes) – a solution of which the evaluation has not been favourable over the last decade: there are still cases pending in the law courts which indicate long-term resistance to enforced territorial crosscutting.

Although adoption of specific models of the local PAS are seen mainly as a 'one-way street' (from west to east), it should not be ignored that new solutions to pressing problems in Brandenburg could soon be part of the options under review in NRW. There is at least some evidence, that council questions in Brandenburg are discussed in the light of possible reactions in NRW ('if we have supported the introduction of "X" in Brandenburg, we cannot easily deny this in NRW'). In terms of the contents of the commune constitution in NRW, it can be expected that the supporters of grass-roots democratic structures will be endorsed by the development in East Germany – which can be seen as a counter-trend to the dominant West German concern with 'efficient city management'. It is not yet possible, though, to formulate a prognosis about the most probable result of this process.

Trends of Regionalization

There are also other trends in NRW (and beyond), which might influence the changes of the commune constitution: for example the regionalization of public tasks. This has been promoted intensively by the state government through setting up various programmes (ZIM, ZIN) for regional development.[15] One central aim was the demand for inter-communal co-operation and priority setting. Regional conferences were set up to propose projects for infrastructure development. This does not automatically imply a 'retreat' of state government in these affairs: it has still kept its power of final decision. Thus it can be asked whether this is just a new strategy to enforce state policies at the local level by building up and using regional institutions with weak democratic legitimacy. It is also noteworthy that these programmes have been 'declared' a success without any serious evaluation taking place.

Although it is difficult to estimate the structural consequences of these initiatives, the parallels with the idea of a 'Europe of regions' may be considered. The dimensions of the conceptualized regions are quite different (much smaller in NRW), but in both debates the general structure of the federal system of democratic legitimation and public administration is the central concern. One model emerging out of this scenario could be the division of labour between regions (political respresentation for planning and guidance) and communes/municipalities (efficient administration, especially management of public services). This perspective could be combined with the propositions for reform of the commune constitution. It opens up another way to the increasingly 'advertised' 'Local Services Ltd' (Städtische Dienste GmbH/AG).[16] Thus, it is quite possible that the future of the commune constitution in NRW will be much more influenced by such 'global' trends than by complaints about, and an evaluation of, the existing model.

CONCLUSIONS

The review of the changes in the communal constitution of NRW since 1946 has revealed a long list of elements which have undergone modification because of specific criticisms: regarding the quality of representation of the citizens' interests, the division of power and responsibilities between political actors and local administration, and so on. This has not led, however, to a general change of the overall model – which could have been quite easily done, because there are working alternatives in Germany. It has been argued that too many interests in all groups and parties would be affected. This would not allow a majority in the state parliament and in the local councils for such a general change. This thesis can also be applied to the recent reform debate and procedure – although alternative (overall) models are brought into the discussion (especially the 'Süddeutsche Ratsverfassung').

Another reason for the expected outcome of this reform debate are the (by no means conclusive) results of a comparative evaluation of different models. Even if one restricts the comparison to very selective criteria, there is considerable variation in performance – depending on several context factors (like size, economy, and so on). This leads to the suggestion that a change of the commune constitution is less important than a sound evaluation of the practice and its evaluation-related improvement. This could also lead to the proposition that the (re-)formulation of the commune constitution should leave more scope for the variations within each state.

Finally, more general trends have been linked to the issues under debate. Forces for change which stem from these trends will probably have the greatest impact on the future 'model' of local politics and administration in NRW. The trend toward a 'Europe of regions' will probably lead to a shift in the distribution of responsibilities and functions between different levels of the German PAS. In this way the communes and municipalities might concentrate much more on efficient administration, whereas on the regional level democratic legitimation, representation, guidance, and control would dominate. It has to be noted, though, that such a scenario is plausible only for western Germany at the moment. In eastern Germany the mainstream goes in the other direction: small units (communes) are seen as the basis for democratic participation and legitimation, whereas co-operative networks and joint institutions should build up a large-sized and efficient administration. It will be a very complicated and lengthy task to find a common basis of commune constitution for the whole of Germany.

NOTES

1. U. Andersen (ed.), *Kommunalpolitik und Kommunalwahlen in NRW* (Landeszentrale für pol. Bildung, 1984); H.U. Erichsen (ed.), *Kommunalverfassung Heute und Morgen – Bilanz und Ausblick* (Carl Heymanns, 1989).
2. P.M. Mombaur, *Gemeindeordnung NRW* (Deutscher Gemeindeverlag, 1986).
3. F. Wagener, *Der Neubau der Verwaltung* (de Gruyter, 1969).
4. H.U. Erichsen (ed.), op.cit.
5. Umfrage zu den Bedingungen der Kommunalpolitik in NRW, Innenministerium, 1990.
6. G. Banner, 'Zur politisch administrativen Steuerung in der Kommune', Archiv für Kommunalwissenschaften (1982), pp. 26–47.
7. R.R. Grauhan, 'Modelle Politischer Verwaltungsführung', Politische Vierteljahresschrift (1969), pp. 269–81.
8. See D.Schimanke (ed.), *Stadtdirekttor oder Bürgermeister* (Basel: Birkhäuser Verlag, 1989).
9. G. Banner in ibid., pp. 37–61.
10. V. Kunz–Zapf and T. Schramm in ibid., pp. 161–89.
11. H. Nassmacher in ibid., pp. 62–83.
12. H.G. Wehling in ibid., pp. 84–96.
13. D. Thränhardt in ibid., pp. 206–17.
14. For a summary see O. Scheytt, 'Verwaltungshilfen für die Kommunen in den neuen Ländern der Bundesrepublik Deutschland', Archiv für Kommunalwissenschaften (1991), pp. 1–10.
15. For a summary see H. Kruse, *Reform durch Regionalisierung* (Campus, 1990).
16. G. Banner, 'Von der Behörde zum Dienstleistungsunternehmen, VOP, January 1991, pp. 6–11.

FIGURE 1
THE STRUCTURE AND PROCESS OF LOCAL GOVERNMENT IN NORDRHEIN–WESTFALIA

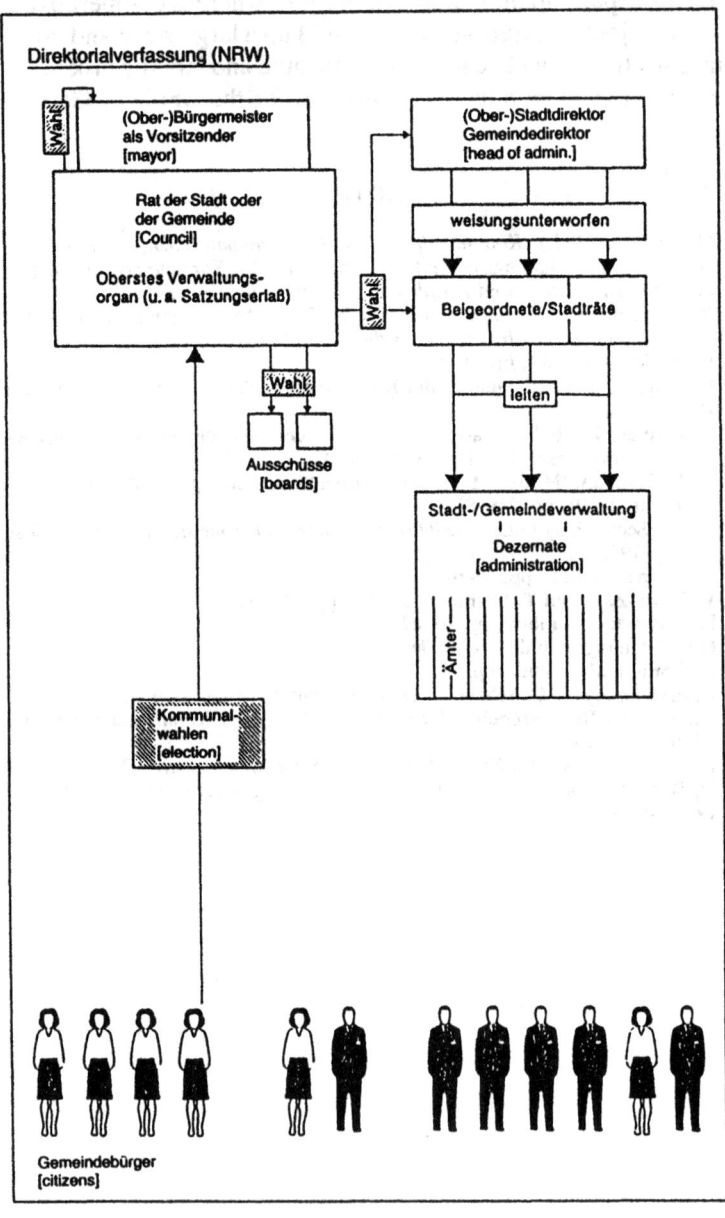

The Relationship between the Political and the Executive Structure in Italian Local Government

GIANCARLO ROLLA

The Italian government, after many long and difficult parliamentary discussions, has passed Act 142 of 1990.[1] Its relevance is due, on the one hand, to the fact that it has awarded a statutory autonomy and wide legislative powers to towns and provinces and, on the other, because it has redefined, by applying new concepts, the political structure of local government and its relationship with bureaucracy.

THE CRISIS OF THE TRADITIONAL PATTERN OF DECISION-MAKING

Act 142 of 1990 has profoundly changed the organization of local government. Previously the law was exclusively geared to the problem of competence, and of the distribution of power between central and local government. It has now made it possible, perhaps for the first time since Italy adopted a republican system of government in 1948, seriously to review the role of local government, the taxation system, and the provision of services. This is a new experience for Italy, allowing it to overcome the traditional apathy of Italian public administration towards verifying the results of its own activity.

The organization of local authorities before Act 142 of 1990 seemed inadequate and it was considered one of the main causes of the poor functioning of local government. Based on Act 148 of 1915 and Act 383 of 1934, it appeared to be incapable of supplying adequately the needs of an efficient and effective administration, as demanded by a complex and fragmented society.

Previous legislation had set up a certain number of political bodies which, on the one hand, were structurally inefficient owing to the lack of real communications within the organization, and, on the other hand, had no specific identity as the law did not define a separate role for each body. This led to the superimposition of powers and some uncertainty and competition over who was to do what. The executive committee (giunta), far from being considered a modern organ of government, was run like an assembly sometimes very large, whose prime task was to substitute for the council (consiglio) in cases of urgent need or to give administrative execution to the resolutions of the council.[2]

The council, in its turn, though it was the main organ and had general functions, was run more like an association of representatives of the electors than as a political assembly in charge of the fundamental administrative policy of the local community. One has only to remember the following two points: firstly, that the old law did not prescribe any form of internal organization of the function of its members, and secondly that it did not allow for very frequent decision making by the council. The practice was for two meetings to be held a year unless there should be need for an exceptional one.

Moreover, the relationship between political power and bureaucracy was completely neglected. It was left to a single figure, that of the mayor, who was seen as the political head of the administration.

This model of organization, applied to modern society and the welfare state, proved to be totally inadequate. It created a weak political structure, operating mainly as an assembly and with its activities rigidly confined to set times. Moreover, from a strictly institutional point of view, the law gave less importance to the smaller executive committee. The result was that the decision-making structure was highly vertical, with the assembly of elected members as the centre of decisions and the mayor as a truly political institution with executive powers.

No wonder, then, that the way local authorities really functioned was very different from the model set by the law. Even before the innovations of Act 142 of 1990, local government was run along different lines from those originally set out. Nor could it have been otherwise when one considers the enormous changes which have taken place in the period before the law came into force. The political structure of society has undergone deep changes due to the rise and growth of political parties, while the functions of local authorities have been modified by the accelerating tendency in all fields to bring the economy and social life under administrative control. Such transformations have progressively moved the centre of political administrative life to the executive committee.

The complexity of the work of the administrators has led to the development of the executive committee as a body which can be counted on to support the bureaucracy's decisions. There had never been a direct relationship between the council and local bureaucracy; contacts had to be filtered through the highest political administrative level, that is, the executive committee, the mayor, or the single councillor politically responsible for a department 'assessore'. This lack of communication had played a decisive role in the process of erosion of the council's powers by the executive committee. It became clear that the administration was not merely implementing or executing the council's deliberations but had itself come to represent the seat of planning and of the processing of information, in other words the preparatory stages of all decisions local authorities have to take.

The growth in importance of the executive committee at the expense of the mayor has been caused by two factors. On the one hand, the heterogeneity of the functions administered by the local authorities has made a monocratic management difficult for a small or medium-sized authority. On the other hand, the development of a multi-party system has led to the institution of coalition governments, which inevitably make the executive committee the centre of the executive, in so much as it is an assembly in which all the forces expressing the political majority in the town council take part.

THE EXECUTIVE COMMITTEE'S ROLE IN GOVERNMENT AND ITS RELATIONSHIP WITH THE COUNCIL

Act 142 of 1990 intends to regulate the relationship between the three main political organs (the council, the executive committee, and the president or mayor) by defining both their powers and their institutional roles. Articles 32 and 35 of this new law, if taken together, help us to define the relationship between the council and the executive committee using three criteria.

(A) In the first place, the powers of the two organs are defined with reference neither to matters on which they can take decisions nor to the value of the matters defined, but to the main function which the law attributes to each of them. The tasks of the council established by Article 32 of Act 142 of 1990 may be classified under five headings, the first two of which are not predeterminable acts but are the expression of general governing activity.

The council has the power to:
1. carry out activities of a political and administrative nature; that is, to take any action or make any decision representing the interests of the community which has elected it; also to pursue the objectives

defined by the electoral manifesto on which the council has gained its own political majority and elected the executive committee and the mayor or president.

2. exercise a political-administrative control over the activity of the executive committee, of the administration and of the services provided. Political control on the work of the executive committee is exercised annually when it presents its report on the year's activity (Article 35) to the full council or by breaking the existing bond of trust which is the consequence of the approval of constructive no confidence (Article 37). Administrative control is effected principally over those officials appointed to direct offices and services: this is in order to check that they are acting in conformity with the council's policy.

3. appoint, choose, or annul the appointment of persons representing the local authority (town or province) in agencies, organizations or institutions operating within the local authority's sphere or dependent on or controlled by it.

4. take measures on certain matters which through their intrinsic importance must be considered a basic activity of the authority, for example, statutes, regulations, plans, financial plans, staff discipline, conventions and agreements with other authorities, tariffs and taxes.

5. deliberate on certain matters which cannot be termed policy-making, but rather concern the process of management and execution, and which, owing to their importance, come under the control of the council, such as mortgage expenses which will go on budgets of successive financial years, the buying of property, and so on

(B) Secondly, the relationship between the council and its executive committee is inverted: the organ with general or residual powers is no longer the council but its committee. According to Article 35 of Act 142 of 1990, the latter has the power to deliberate on all matters which the law or the statutes do not consider the prerogative either of the council or of the mayor or the president of the province, the decentralized bodies, the secretary, or the officials.

It follows that the committee is the political organ of local government defined by Act 142 of 1990 in more innovatory terms.

In the first place, the new system of local autonomy has given it the characteristics of a modern organ of government. Both its functional profile and its organizational structure have been improved.

Secondly, Act 142 of 1990, realistically taking into account past experience, was intended to safeguard the functioning of the authority from being seriously hampered by political instability, delays in the constitution of its bodies and recurrent crises.

Article 34 has fixed binding times for the election of the mayor, the president of the province, and the respective committees, with the aim of avoiding the difficulties in constituting executive bodies, which could occur in the present situation dominated by 'coalition governments':[3] nonetheless, the best way to ensure the stability of the organ of government would perhaps have been to pass a new electoral law correcting proportional representation, so as to favour an immediate formation of a majority and of one or more oppositions.

In the light of long experience in comparative jurisprudence, Article 27 introduces the practice of constructive no-confidence. As a result crises will be less likely to occur since compulsory resignations have been tied to the approval of a specific motion of constructive no-confidence, containing 'the proposal of new political and administrative policies, a new mayor or president of the province and a new committee'.

Lastly, the legislation has rightly emphasized the unity of the executive organ by indissolubly binding the life of the committee to the term of office of its president: the resignation, end of term of office or death of the latter cause the inevitable end of the former. This is how the legislators have transformed Article 157 of the Act of 1915, which gave the senior councillor the right to exercise the functions of mayor or president, even in the case of a vacancy of office owing to resignation or permanent impediment.

The function of the monocratic organ of local government (the mayor or the president) has not really been altered by Act 142 of 1990. The most important changes have been introduced through the statutes of some local authorities, which, in the hope of reducing the conditioning of coalition governments, have envisaged a form of parliamentary government led by a president. While, on the one hand, the council formulates its plans on the basis of the demands of the local community and, on the other, the committee operates as the organ of government, the mayor or the president becomes the titular head and director of its policies. It is in his or her power to assure that political activity is unified and is coherent and also to take up any initiative which might help the executive to carry out the governmental programme.

Thirdly, the legislation has distributed powers on two tiers: (1) among the political bodies of the authority and (2) between the political bodies and the bureaucratic structure. In the first case, a distinction has been drawn between the council, considered as a policy-making organ and one which exercises political and administrative control, and the committee, empowered by the 1990 Act to carry into effect the general lines of the administration and to ensure the government of the authority. In the second case, the officials appointed to direct offices and services have been given the basic responsibility of their management and of the fulfilment of the objectives set by the elected bodies.

The new Act has made it possible to appoint members of the committee from outside the council. The aim is to raise the quality of decision-making and to combine the political and professional abilities of the members of this body and for this purpose people with technical skills and qualifications are chosen. Two conditions must be respected, however: the first, that this possibility must be approved by the statute of the local authority; the second, that the aspiring person must be qualified to be a councillor. The presence on the committee of non-elected councillors renders the existing difference between the council and its executive body more evident. This is because only the council is a policy-making organ, and must therefore be connected with the electorate it represents. Since, instead, the function of the committee is that of putting policy into effect, the political conditioning of its members can be off-set by the introduction of qualified people with professional skills who can contribute to a successful administration.

THE DISTINCTION BETWEEN THE DUTIES OF THE POLITICAL ORGANS AND THOSE OF OFFICIALS: THE POWER OF OFFICIALS

The most significant innovation introduced in Article 51 of Act 142 of 1990 is doubtless the attribution of special powers to officials, by differentiating between the duties of the administration and those pertaining to the political body.

Article 51 makes an important contribution towards the definition of the duties and the role of public officials. Even though it specifies that statutes and regulations of the single authorities must be consulted for a more detailed application, it has separated, according to functions, the political bodies from those of the officials. To the former it falls to fix objectives, decide on the political and administrative lines and see that they are put into practice; while the latter hold a managerial responsibility for the fulfilment of the objectives fixed by the organ of the authority, and for the running of offices and of services.

Secondly, Article 51 of the Local Authority Act assigns specific duties and functions of extra-local government relevance also. Among these the most important is the chairmanship of selection boards both for positions and for tenders. This is an important, innovatory attribution which breaks away from the principle which goes back to the 1853 law concerning public administration. This stated that all the duties of the administrative staff were the responsibility of the political leaders and the staff discharged them not as part of their own responsibilities but as delegates of political power. By giving autonomous standing to the posts to which officials are appointed the legislation has set one of the conditions which enable officials to discharge their functions in an independent and responsible way.

On the one hand Article 51.2 of Act 142 of 1990 has laid down that it is officials who must be at the head of offices and services, according to the principles contained in the statutes and regulations. On the other hand, Article 51.3 of the same law says that officials must carry out all duties including the adoption of those decisions which involve those external affairs which have not been specified as pertaining to the governing bodies of the authority by the law or the statutes.

In connection with the direction of offices and services on the part of officials, the statutes that have shown greater courage in differentiating political control from administrative management, have generally empowered officials to:

- administer budget allocations;
- organize office work;
- manage the staff appointed;
- adopt extraordinary measures relative to the staff;
- actuate internal mobility of the staff;
- create or merge groups working together within the structure.

In conformity with this system of distribution of powers the most recent contract concerning rates of pay and conditions of service of personnel employed by territorial local authorities (D.P.R. 268 of 1977) has recognized that officials are empowered and responsible for the management of the funds used to improve the efficiency of services; to this end they have been given managerial powers in determining financial incentives for productivity *(Fondo per il miglioramento dell'efficienza dei servizi)*, overtime and working hours.

As far as defining the responsibility of officials over staff matters is concerned, reference must be made to certain specific problems inherent in pay disputes since, according to Act 93 1983,[4] these disputes concern the employee's role or status and hence the productivity and efficiency of the departments and services. This, as we have seen before, is closely connected with the managerial function of officials.

Officials, in so far as they are responsible for the running of the departments and services, are responsible also for administrative procedures. They must ensure the transparency of the decision-making process, the participation of all interests involved in the administrative process, the attainment of the political objectives set by the executive committee or by the council and the rationality and efficiency of the administration.[5]

However, where acts of external import are concerned, it must be remembered that the executive committee has general competence.[6] The powers of the officials, thus, coincide with the tasks that single authorities have expressly decided, by law or statute, to reserve to them: according to the ratio of the law (Act 142 of 1990) officials should be competent to take any decision which results in putting into effect the general measures proposed by the political bodies.

Lastly, since officials are an important connecting link between political bodies and the bureaucratic structure, it is up to them to provide the former with a continuous flow of necessary, exhaustive information. Officials operate in two directions. They have to see that the policy and plans of the organs of government are put into operation by the administration and, on the other hand, on the basis of their effective experience in the administration, they have to offer the political organs the information necessary to define the choices and objectives of the authority. In other words, officials must monitor the good functioning of offices and services. This can be done by specific informative reports on the state of administrative procedures, the state of progress of programmes approved by the executive committee or the council, staff organization, the proposals to overcome inefficiencies or irregularities that may have been discovered.

THE INSTITUTIONAL ROLE OF OFFICIALS

The institutional role of officials is determined both by the powers which they exercise and by the way they exercise those powers. The former define the function, the latter the role. It is important to underline this distinction as the status of officials not only requires the discharge of particular functions, but also the possession of particular managerial capacities. In fact, in order to be completely successful in a managerial role, certain techniques must be used which indicate a particular ability to make use of all available resources. This is what we mean by the professional ability of an official: a quality which is the sum of a profound experience of the workings of his/her department (tasks, functions, procedures, and so on) and managerial skill in shaping the organization, and in managing the resources with a view to reaching the pre-established objectives. To be a successful official requires the capacity to control relations between processes internal and external to the organization; to make use of resources in the structure, combining them with the real or potential requests coming from the outside world; to organize the work and take decisions in an independent way; to act as a leader and, at the same time, to be able to create amongst the staff of the structure to which one is appointed a feeling of solidarity and shared responsibility. This, in fact, is why the articles relating to the powers of officials specify that in discharging their functions they must aim at ensuring efficiency, productivity, and the economy of the administration.

The widening of their powers tends to make the position of officials working in local authorities comparable to that of their counterparts in the private sector, even more so by Article 51 of Act 142 of 1990 which states, in contrast to the previous Act, that officials can be recruited from outside the public administration and also that they may be appointed with a temporary contract, even with a non-public contract.

However, not all characteristics of officials working in the private sector can be mechanically applied to the public sector. The status of the former is generally thought to be characterized by the following:

(1) a function of policy-making in and coordination of productive activity;
(2) a relationship of trust with the general manager;
(3) powers of representation;
(4) a solid position in the hierarchical structure of the company with powers of supremacy, of organization, and of participation in the management of the company, limited to the sphere of the general directives imparted by the managers and by the representative bodies of the concern.

It is evident that some of these characteristics also belong to the role of the public official. This is especially true of points 1, 3, and 4.

Obviously point 2, a personal relationship of trust with the political leadership is not possible: if it existed, it would be in contrast with the articles of the constitution relating to administrative impartiality. One must also consider the different conditions required to become an official (in the public sector, generally through competition or a selection process, according to existing regulations), and also the fact that the powers of supremacy and of decision-making enjoyed by public officials must always be fully respectful of the principles established by the law.

Moreover, the managing activity of officials in local government cannot be performed fully but is conditioned and hampered by certain rigidities of the system which Act 142 of 1990 has not removed. One must take into consideration that officials discharge their new functions in a structure that is old and rigidly predetermined. Another factor which can equally condition the full performance of managerial activity is the complex discipline which limits both internal and external mobility. This regulation, widely applied in other spheres, has always been looked upon with suspicion by Italian legislators; they seem inclined to guarantee the permanence of employees and to favour the development of their career within the same organization. Such choice tends to favour a practical understanding of the sector rather than managerial ability in the running of a complex structure.

NOTES

1. This fulfils the promise of a general Act of the Republic to define the guiding functions and principles of the autonomy of local government.
2. According to Article 137 of Act 148 of 1915 the executive committee represented the council between meetings, took part in the formal functions, supervised the running of local services, making sure that the council's decisions were held firm.
3. The executive committee must be elected within 60 days following the result of the election of the concil or, in the case of resignation, from the date on which this has been presented. The council will otherwise be dissolved and new elections called.
4. This Act states the general principles on matters of public employment to which all public administration must comply.
5. according to Article 4 of Act 241 of 1990 (on administrative proceedings), for every kind of proceeding the public administration must define the unit internal to its organization which is to be responsible for the preliminary investigation and for every other stage in the execution and also for the adoption of the final decision.

European Influence on Local Self-Government?

COLIN CRAWFORD

The European Charter of Local Self-Government is the first multilateral legal instrument to define and safeguard the principles of local autonomy, one of the pillars of democracy which it is the Council of Europe's function to defend and develop.[1]

Local government is not a suitable subject for regulation by an international convention.[2]

INTRODUCTION

The two European special issues of this journal are concentrating on three important themes in local government. The legal basis of the first two, namely finance and the relationship of political and executive structures, is fundamental and subject to continuing political debate in Great Britain, a debate which has in recent years manifested itself in regard to the legal powers for the third theme, economic development. It is not the intention here to review that debate within Great Britain but, instead, to examine the possibility of external influence over these aspects. This paper approaches the issues from two perspectives. First, from the principles articulated in the European Charter of Local Self-Government, drawn up within the Council of Europe and opened to signature as a convention in 1985.[3] Secondly, from the perspective of the importance of 1992 with regard to local government. In the light of the aims of the Charter, the position in Great Britain is analysed to show how the British position falls short of the ideals articulated therein. Potential solutions to the British position from a legal perspective and other jurisdictions are analysed, and the question raised as to whether the effects of 1992 make the aims of the Charter more or less desirable and possible.

THE CHARTER

Starting from the assumption that the Council of Europe, as the custodian of human rights and the upholder of the principles of democratic government, was the obvious vehicle for the drafting of such a Charter, a new initiative was taken in 1981 by the Standing Conference of Local and Regional Authorities of Europe (CLRAE). The purpose of the resulting Charter 'is to make good the lack of common European standards for measuring and safeguarding the rights of local authorities, which are closest to the citizen and give him the opportunity of participating effectively in the making of decisions affecting his everyday environment'. In the words of the report,

> The Charter commits the parties to applying basic rules guaranteeing the political, administrative and financial independence of local authorities.... it embodies the conviction that the degree of self-government enjoyed by local authorities may be regarded as a touchstone of genuine democracy. (p. 8)

Any such attempt to develop basic rules had to confront the diversity and range of institutional arrangements which already existed in Europe. While seeking to harmonize these in regard to the fundamental aspects, some room had to be left for differences of approach. As the report stated, the necessary flexibility to take account of the differences between national constitutional arrangements and administrative traditions was to be built in, 'not by excessively diluting the requirements of the new instruments but by allowing governments a degree of choice with regard to the provisions by which they would consider themselves bound' (p. 6).

The way in which this was to be achieved was by dividing the main body of the Charter into two parts. Part I contains the substantive provisions setting out the principles of local self-government, specifying the need for a constitutional and legal foundation, and defining and establishing the principles governing the nature and scope of local authorities' power. Part II, however, permits the parties to exclude certain provisions from those by which they will be bound. This is achieved by requiring each party to consider itself bound by at least 20 of the 30 paragraphs in Part I, at least ten of which must be drawn from a list of the 14 most important.

The 11 Articles in Part I cover the constitutional and legal foundation for local self-government; the concept of local self-government; the scope of local self-government; protection of local authority boundaries; appropriate administrative structures and resources; conditions under which responsibilities at local level are exercised; administrative supervision of local authorities' activities; financial resources of local authorities; local authorities' right to associate; and legal protection of local self-government.

While all are important in some way, the two core provisions are Article 4, relating to the scope of local self-government, and Article 9 dealing with the financial resources of local authorities. Although the signatory governments are technically not obliged to include these provisions within those by which they consider themselves bound, the intention behind the Charter was that, once a signatory, any government would find it increasingly difficult to justify why these two most important elements were not accepted.

As the explanatory report points out, Article 4 lays down the general principles on which the responsibilities of local authorities and the nature of their powers should be based. The core of Article 4 lies in paragraph 2, which requires the authority to be given what is termed 'general competence'. This means that, in addition to specific responsibilities and duties, the authority should have the right to exercise initiative in matters which they consider to promote the general welfare of their inhabitants. Equally, in regard to Article 9, it is pointed out that the 'legal authority to perform certain functions is meaningless if local authorities are deprived of the financial resources to carry them out' (p. 16). Thus the provisions seek to ensure that the authority is not deprived of its freedom to determine exenditure priorities, to obtain adequate resources for its tasks, part of which should be raised locally at a level determined by the authority, and that the sources of finance are responsive to economic changes and not tied to specific projects or courses of action.

At present, 18 national governments have signed the Charter and 12 have ratified it. The United Kingdom has failed to sign, the only other governments in this position being Hungary (which acceded to the Council of Europe only in November 1990), Ireland, Malta, San Marino, and Switzerland. In regard to the ability to limit, under Part II, the provisions applying to those national governments which have ratified, Sir Duncan Lock, the Vice-Chairman of the Council Committee on Structures, Finance and Management, concluded in May 1990 that 'some have used this flexibility in a modest way whilst others have not needed to do so'.

The British government, however, show no signs of signing. In addition to the statement of Michael Portillo, the minister quoted at the start of this paper, the government recently stated in the House of Lords that they had no plans to sign the Charter.[4] In that short debate, when pressed by Lord Rippon, a former Conservative government minister, to follow the example of other countries and sign the Charter, Baroness Blatch, the government minister, argued that the British were at least honest in stating that certain of the articles were unacceptable, implying that other countries were lacking in this honesty in that they did not actually implement the Charter despite signing or ratifying it.

In order to understand why the key provisions are unacceptable to the British government and thus a barrier to what the Council of Europe sees as a necessary harmonization of institutional arrangements it is necessary to understand a little of the legal framework of local government in Great Britain.

THE LEGAL STATUS OF LOCAL GOVERNMENT IN BRITAIN

The position of local government in Great Britain cannot be explained in detail in a paper of this nature. However, a crude summary of the main elements can be made to allow an examination of the general principles on which the nature of the powers of local authorities, and their financial resources, are based. Given the lack of a written constitution in the normal sense, there is a problem in theorizing about the British constitution and drawing firm conclusions about what is constitutional.[5] This has been seen in the debates over whether recent events in regard to fundamental changes in the law relating to local government have been 'unconstitutional'. Approaching this historically shows that there have been contradictions and ambiguity in both political and legal analysis. At the political level, the question has been seen as central authority or democratic pluralism? At the legal level the debate is couched in terms of the choice between the extremes of parliamentary sovereignty or residual prerogative and discretion.

In terms of legal analysis, it must be stated firmly at the outset that following the reorganization of local government in the 1970s, all local authorities, with the minor exception of the City of London, are now created by statute so they have no protected status and, in legal theory, parliament can add to or reduce their powers simply by passing any other piece of legislation. This formal legal position was invoked by the Conservative government in the early 1980s in the form of the 'unitary state' theory by which the restrictions on local authority tax raising were justified, contrary to established conventions and understandings. The subordinate position of local government is maintained through a variety of methods of control available to central government in relation to local government, the main methods of which can be briefly summarized as legislative (through both primary and delegated legislation): financial (through borrowing and capital controls, and grants and revenue control); circulars (which can in many cases be binding in practice); directions on particular cases or issues; inspection and inquiries; default; and the use of quangos to remove functions form local authority control.

This position of extensive control, based on a strict adherence to the pure view of the concept of parliamentary sovereignty, is not without its critics and it is no coincidence that the proponents of a Bill of Rights for Britain, while disgreeing on many of the rights to be protected by such a document, agree that the position of local government should be protected under any such Bill. However, it is not necessary to reject or modify the doctrine of Parliamentary sovereignty to point out that the traditional view of the legal position of local government in Britain has always been more complicated and richer than the simple idea of the 'unitary state' implies. Five aspects illustrate the point that parliamentary sovereignty as a legal concept can coexist with a legal framework which allows local authorities general discretion.

The Residual 'Prerogative'

It had been accepted that the authorities established by Royal Charter, since they acted for the Crown within their geographical area, had freedom under prerogative to act in any way to benefit the inhabitants of their area, provided that the powers had not been reduced by parliament. However, during the 19th century the influence of centralism and the classical economic theory was seen in a number of pieces of legislation, and Parliament restricted the ability of local authorities to spend money on matters other than those which were authorized by statute. Thus in *Attorney-General v. Manchester Corporation*[6] it was held that the prerogative power was in practice suspended, since without expenditure the ability to spend in any other ways to benefit the inhabitants of their area was illusory. In the present century, however, the role of the public sector was subject to much debate and there was a rise of municipal socialism. The Local Government Act 1933, which consolidated the previous legislation, omitted the restriction on expenditure only on these matters which were authorized by statute, although whether by oversight or conscious design is unclear. This resulted in the case of *Attorney-General v. Leicester Corporation*[7] where the existence of the prerogative was reasserted. In Scotland the equivalent powers of the burghs under the 'common good' funds were transferred to the new statutory authorities in 1975 and continue to the present day, with substantial assets owned by some cities. While the practical importance of this residual prerogative in England and Wales was always limited, in that many of the local authorities such as county councils were created by statute and so were not affected by this debate, following the abolition of all charter authorities at reorganization this issue is no longer of any immediate practical importance. It does, however, serve to undermine the simple 'unitary state' thesis which has so dominated the thinking of central government since 1979.

The Use of Private Acts

Local authorities have always been able to seek additional powers from parliament, and it was through this legal device that local authorities in the 19th century undertook the development of their services of lighting, water, drainage, and gas. Although it can be pointed out that the discretion did not therefore lie with the local authority, but with parliament, it must be noted that this was in a period when there was less domination of parliament by the executive, and before there was the necessity for devices to be created to alleviate the pressure on parliamentary time. Now, such devices are controlled by central government rather than being given to the local authorities and made subject to some other control. While private bills are still used in the British system, and much economic development activity took place under the authority of these Acts, they are a cumbersome and inefficient device, as evidenced by the recent experience with the Cardiff Bay Barrage Bill. The current proposals to streamline the procedures will affect public utilities only, not local authorities.[8]

The Royal Commissions' Views

The role of the local authority in the post-war period increased, which emphasized the complexity of the types and powers of local authorities and need for rationalization, and Royal Commissions were established to review the position. The Royal Commission on Local Government in England tried to balance the different elements and difficulties in doing this. In attempting to combine the elements of efficiency, democracy and the belief in general all-purpose authorities, the Commission examined the effect of the *ultra vires* principle on local authorities. This principle, of course, means that the authorities can do only those things which are expressly or impliedly authorized by an Act of Parliament. The Commission concluded that the need to find positive authority for any proposed course of action, and the threat of legal and financial sanctions for the breach of the principle of *ultra vires*, meant that innovative ideas were inhibited and efficient, responsive delivery of services was not encouraged. A power of general competence was therefore advocated to allow authorities to do anything which was not prohibited. This view was also accepted by the equivalent Royal Commission for Scotland, which thought that the more liberal legal framework would create 'an enterprising and forward looking attitude of mind'. This recommendation was not accepted in the resulting Local Government Act 1972, or Local Government (Scotland) Act 1973, even in the face of powerful pressure being exerted during the legislative debates. Despite the outcome, this emphasizes that the idea of a power of general competence is not seen as completely alien to the British approach.

The 'Free Two Pence' Experiment

Although a power of general competence was not given to local authorities, s.137 of the Local Government Act 1972 and s.83 of the Local Government (Scotland) Act 1973 established a limited general spending power. Known colloquially as the 'free two pence' from the fact that the original financial limit was the product of the two pence rate for the authority, the power authorizes authorities to incur expenditure in any manner which they consider will benefit some or all of the inhabitants of their area. Legally, the power created numerous problems because one of the restrictions was that it was not to be available where another power authorized or prohibited the expenditure. Given the uncertainty over the *ultra vires* doctrine, there were genuine problems over the availability of this power.

It is fair to say that the pattern of expenditure under the power was erratic, with most of the money being spent on economic development powers, although some of the other expenditure generated controversy far beyond its financial significance. Having initially attempted to stop local authorities engaging in economic development activities, on the basis that it was a national issue, the government was frustrated by the availability of this power. Over the years, however, the sum available was not increased with inflation and eventually, in the Local Government and Housing Act 1989, under the guise of 'giving' a new functional power to local government, the government specifically authorized local government to engage in economic development, but only under the very restrictive terms of that Act. It also has to be noted that expenditure controls reduced much of the utility of such a power. However, it is an important symbol for the local government world which again counters the simple 'unitary state' thesis.

Other Methods of Legal Flexibility

Too narrow an application of the *ultra vires* principle would make local government unworkable. Many situations occur where proposed courses of action would not be authorized but where a 'common-sense' rather than legalistic view would consider the action acceptable. Various devices exist in the British system to deal with such situations and introduce much-needed flexibility to the system. Two of these can be seen in relation to the operation of the control through the auditor, in practice the main legal check on the spending of local authorities. The Local Government Finance Act 1982, s.19(1) provides that

> Where it appears to the auditor carrying out the audit of any accounts under this part of the Act that any item of account is contrary to law he may apply to the court for a declaration that the item is contrary to law except where it is sanctioned by the Secretary of State.

Thus, the auditor has a discretion whether to seek a remedy against unlawful expenditure. In practice, this discretion not to take action is exercised regularly. Similarly, stemming from the time when the auditor did not possess this discretion, but was required to disallow all unlawful expenditure, a sanction may be obtained from the central government minister under this section. In this way, expenditure which is clearly unlawful can be undertaken. Applications for sanctions under this power are not infrequent, there being a matter of hundreds each year, although most are minor applications.

WIDER POWERS FOR LOCAL GOVERNMENT?

It is clear from the above brief description that the constitutional position is more complicated, and the need of efficient local government for flexibility more pressing, than the simple view of the 'unitary state' and the doctrine of *ultra vires* would allow. For many, the logic of the need for flexibility and innovation would lead to the implementation of the Charter and the establishment of a power of general competence. Yet, at least in central government, the simple view still prevails and there remains much misunderstanding of the nature of a power of general competence.

As recently as January 1990 the idea of general competence was again rejected. In the context of whether the government would sign the Charter, Baroness Blatch stated that 'the Government objects to the powers of general competence ... [it] ... means that local authorities would be empowered to do absolutely anything they wished outside the provisions proscribed by Parliament'.[9] Such a view misunderstands the nature of the judicially created doctrine of *ultra vires*. The judicial principles of abuse of power would remain in relation to a power of general competence, and doubts must be expressed about the willingness of the judiciary to shed their restrictive approach to local government if such a power was enacted. The most that would change is the presumption of legality, and it is not a fundamentally different doctrine. Indeed, as indicated below in relation to the Scandinavian jurisdictions, while operating within the formal principle of general competence it is possible to have very tight restrictions, and it is far from the case that authorities either can or would wish to do 'absolutely anything'. Since that rejection, the Secretary of State has established a review of local government, known as the 'Heseltine review'. This includes for discussion the question 'what is the case for a power of general competence?'. While the formal position is therefore that the matter remains open, it is unlikely that the government will accept the adoption of the principle.

Instead, another method is being advocated by the Local Authority Associations, and others, as more acceptable politically to the government, and therefore with more chance of being introduced. Ironically, it is wider in its implications than the introduction of a power of general competence and as a result may be considered appropriate for introduction in all European countries which have adopted the aims of the Charter. This is the experiment in Scandinavian countries known as the 'Free Local Government' experiment. A brief examination of the Norwegian experiment will serve to illustrate the basic nature of the different schemes.[10]

Although Norwegian local authorities have a power of general competence, many of their activities are carried out on the basis of duties imposed on them. The experiment is seen as one of a number of reforms in regard to local government, reflecting the trend to decentralization and an emphasis on effectiveness, not only in regard to powers which the authority takes under the power of general competence, but also those which are subject to national legislation. As the scheme is described by its coordinator,

> The core of the free local government scheme is that some local government units, on application, may be exempted from existing legislation, which they feel hamper an adjustment of policy, services and administration to local conditions. Instead the councils determine their own alternative by-laws, subject to

approval by the Ministry of Local Government. Thus, they are given the opportunity to adapt national standards for task-solving and organisational patterns to local conditions, on initiative from the local councils themselves.[11]

The experiment has been in existence since 1986, and is likely to result in a permanent tool of innovation being given to local government in Norway. In relation to its applicability to Britain, it should be noted that applications in Norway are made to the ministry. This is seen by many as unworkable in Britain and it has been suggested that the power to allow such applications should be given to a new joint select committee of parliament.[12] If further evidence is needed of the merits of this view, it can be seen from the Norwegian experience in terms of what innovations have been introduced under the experiment, where Lodden states that three categories of projects have dominated:

> Firstly, projects focusing on economic development policies. Secondly, projects concentrating on the organisation of the educational system and adjacent services directed at children and youngsters. Thirdly, projects concerning the local government organisation and political management in general.

While this emphasized that the same issues are important in regard to local government in different jurisdictions, it should be noted that these three issues have been very controversial in Britain in recent years but have been subject to increased central control. In economic development issues, as explained above, the main discretionary spending power of local government was used to introduce a wide variety of effective schemes which were accepted as being very successful, many of which are now no longer allowed following the Local Government and Housing Act 1989. In regard to educational provision, the thrust of central government policy under the Education Reform Act 1988 is to reduce the involvement of local government by allowing schools to 'opt out' of local government and be funded by the centre, by taking further education out of local control, and the possibility of taking all education expenditure out of local government budgets is on the political agenda at present. In regard to local government organization, the government set up a committee of inquiry, and the legislative response to this has been termed the 'de-politicization of local government'.[13]

The major problem with this proposal to borrow and adapt the Scandinavian experiment, apart from whether there is the necessary political will at the local level and the question of central control, is the problem of finance. Indeed, that is a problem for all jurisdictions and the Charter. To understand this limitation we need to examine the financial position of local government in Britain.

LOCAL GOVERNMENT FINANCE IN BRITAIN

No explanation in a paper such as this can allow an understanding of all the complexities of the system, and the numerous schemes of local government finance which have been in operation since 1979. Instead, it is the intention to highlight the main aspects of these only, in order that the extent of influence of central control through financial controls at present can be appreciated, and an assessment made of the contention that a fundamental change has taken place in relation to the status of local government within our constitutional arrangements.

The system is based on both capital and revenue controls. On the revenue side the income of local authorities was composed mainly of the income from central government grants and from the rates, a property tax based on the notional rental value of the property. The old grant system was based on a combination of three factors – needs, resources and domestic subsidy elements. Grants were either specific or general. The rating system was based on domestic and commercial rates. In general, the proportions of the two had altered in the post-war period, with grants rising from 40 per cent to nearly 60 per cent of income.

Crudely, the interaction between the local revenue raising and central support systems meant there could be an incentive for authorities to spend more in order to obtain more support grant. This resulted, as economic factors were considered paramount, in the move to expenditure targets and restrictions, first established in law under the Local Government Planning and Land Act 1980. This process reversed the trend to increase the proportion of the grant element, as central government attempted to reduce expenditure by reducing grants to a level based on centrally determined expenditure levels. However, as each system proved ineffective in controlling local government expenditure, new legislation was introduced to establish additional controls and restrict the ability of local authorities to decide their own expenditure levels. Crucial stages in this process were the abolition of supplementary rates or precepts issued during the financial year after the grant allocation had been determined, and 'hold-back' mechanisms for grants to penalize 'overspenders'. When even these failed, and some authorities were receiving no grant whatsoever, direct rate control and 'rate-capping' were introduced by the Rates Act

1984. Thus local authorities were not only subject to the discretion of central government as to how much, or little, grant would be received, but they were no longer able to determine the yield from their local tax base.

The rating system had been criticized on a number of grounds and various alternatives were put forward. However despite various suggestions, and an official report, the Layfield Committee of Inquiry, advocating a local income tax, no reforms had been introduced. The government, however, were committed to reform the system of local taxation. This eventually resulted, with a great deal of controversy, in the Local Government Finance Act 1988 which introduced a radically different system.

Rates were retained, in an amended, centrally controlled form, for non-domestic property. Thus local authorities could no longer determine the tax burden on commercial activities within their area. Rates on domestic property, however, were abolished in favour of a tax on individuals, formally designated the 'community charge' but better known as the 'poll tax', which is not related to income. The main justification stated at the time for this was to increase accountability to the voters for spending decisions. Given the necessary reduction in the proportion of revenue to be raised by local government, however, it would be a mistake to see it as anything other than part of the continuing atttempt to reduce local authority expenditure, an aim now admitted by the government as a reason for, in turn, abolishing the unpopular 'poll tax' which proved impossible to administer.

The income of local authorities is at present largely obtained from the three sources of non-domestic rate, grants from central government, and the community charge. Only in regard to the latter does the local authority have any discretion as to the amount to be raised, but it should be noted that despite the stated aim of increasing accountability, the government had, and exercised, the power to substitute their own view for this discretion and 'cap' the level of 'poll tax' for any authority. Even for those authorities not subjected to the capping process, the change to the poll tax meant that from being able to determine the level of taxation for 50 per cent of their income, the authority could exercise discretion over only 20 per cent. Even that element is now under threat. As a result of the unpopularity of the poll tax, the government have now reduced the levels of charges by transferring a fixed amount to central funds, to be raised by an increase in value added tax, raising the question of whether it is any longer worthwhile to have a local taxation system. In this regard it is interesting to note that the Chartered Institute of Public Finance and Accountancy and the Audit Commission have both stated that the yield from the tax is no longer justified by the collection costs, if the proportion remains at the present level. Whatever new system is introduced to replace the poll tax, this issue will have to be addressed.

In addition to the revenue controls, in the general attempt to impose central control there have been important changes in the system of capital controls which, despite some of the earlier schemes failing to be wholly successful, have clearly constrained the freedom of local authority action. In response to these statutory limitations there was the emergence of 'creative accounting' and increased recourse to the courts by local authorities. Some of these devices were notorious and difficult to defend on grounds of other than short-term revenue raising, such as the lease and leaseback schemes applied to town halls and other assets even down to parking meters, while others were more debatable.[14] Under the new system introduced by the Local Government and Housing Act 1989, a very effective, if highly complex, system of control has been given to central government.

WILL THE CHARTER SUCCEED?

This question can be addressed in two ways. First, whether the British position is likely to change as a result of internal pressure. Secondly, whether other pressures from external sources, particularly the Community institutions, will strengthen the status of the Charter and make it more difficult for the British to ignore its provisions.

On the domestic front, pressure is growing within the local government world for the Charter to be signed. In response to the request to sign or at least include the issue in the 'Heseltine review', Baroness Blatch, the government minister in the House of Lords, replied that 'the Government have no plans to sign the Charter. . . . As regards the review, nothing is ruled in and nothing is ruled out'.

The fact that the review has not excluded the possibility has encouraged local government to raise the matter again. However, mindful of the previously expressed view of the government that local government is not a suitable subject for regulation by an international convention, and that the specific question of signing was not included in the 21 main, or 103 subsidiary, questions set out by the review for discussion, the local authority associations are approaching the task indirectly.

In March 1991, they issued a joint statement entitled 'Principles of Local Government'.[15] This statement lays down a number of principles under five general headings. Many of the principles owe much, and are expressed in similar terms, to those in the Charter. Thus, there is a principle that 'local authorities should have a power of general competence to act on behalf of local communities on all matters not specifically excluded or assigned to any other authority, subject to the primacy always of basic civil rights and Parliament'. Equally, the principles on local expenditure and taxation assert the right of local government to determine their own level of expenditure and taxation; to have a sufficient tax base to cover a significant proportion of their income; and to operate within a grant system which is primarily an equalizing system, not one intended to restrict the freedom of local government.

All this may appear to raise the possibility of the British government coming into line with the Charter in the near future. It is also interesting to note that British delegations to Hungary, Poland and Bulgaria, under the authority of central government, have urged those countries to adopt the Charter! While of course nothing can be said to be impossible, adoption by the British government is nevertheless extremely unlikely. It would require a complete reversal of the developments of the last 12 years, and is likely to be in direct opposition to the plans for central government to take education and housing away from local authority control. Indeed, when those two functions are removed, and the legislation is implemented fully to require contracts for many services to be given to the private sector if the bid is lower than the local authorities' own costs, local government may have a residual regulatory role only. While such bodies could be given a power of general competence, or some other less restrictive legal framework, financial freedom is not one that is likely to be given easily in Britain. As the relevant Council of Europe Committee noted recently, in the period since the Charter was operative, for financial matters 'there are restrictions on local autonomy (particularly in the United Kingdom and Scandinavian countries) not only through restrictions on revenue but also, and perhaps more importantly, in the form of increasingly stringent controls on local expenditure by central government'.[16]

Attention must therefore turn to whether the British government will be forced to respond to external pressure, whether direct or indirect. As Sir Duncan Lock, the vice-chairman of the relevant Council committee has stated,

> local government in Europe has a charter couched in positive terms and with the status of a European Convention, standing alongside such other important Conventions as the European

Convention of Human Rights and the European Social Charter. But encouraging as this may be, CLRAE still has the twin tasks of persuading every state in Europe to sign and ratify the Charter and of convincing the European Community to recognise and adopt it.[17]

In regard to the second task, in March 1988 the CLRAE passed a resolution inviting three things:

(i) the Commission of the EC to incorporate the key provisions of the Charter in Community legislation;
(ii) the European Parliament to incorporate the principles in the future European constitution;
(iii) the Commission of the EC to co-operate and consult with regional and local representatives on matters concerning their responsibilities.

No response has been forthcoming on the first two requests, but a consultative council has been established for discussions between the local authorities of the member states and the Commission, and has now been in existence for two years. Although this is not a formal institution within the EC its role is a developing one.

There is no doubt that the link between EC powers and the local authorities is becoming greater in terms of substantive issues. On the one hand, it has been pointed out, in a recent Council of Europe report, that by completing the internal market, powers will be transferred to the European level, 'reinforcing trends towards supranational decision-making and curtailing local and regional autonomy in specific fields'.[18] On the other hand, Europe has sometimes found it useful to bypass recalcitrant central governments of member states and deal directly with local governments, such as in the area of regional assistance. Indeed, as central regulation and the setting of common standards increases, the greater the need for diversity and responsiveness at the local level. This is likely to raise questions of principle in due course. As was pointed out in the report, the move towards more supranational powers at the European level emphasizes the question of 'subsidiarity' and the appropriate level of government at which functional powers should be allocated. This is an important question for the division between the responsibilities of the EC and the member states, but it is also a principle of the Charter, under Article 4.3, that public functions should be allocated to the level closest to the citizen wherever possible. Thus the conclusion was reached that the

> new Council could be an appropriate forum for marrying the two levels of discussion on subsidiarity, i.e. the allocation of func-

tional powers between the E.C. and central governments on the one hand and central government and subnational authorities on the other hand.[19]

Whether these external influences force the British government to reverse recent developments will partly depend on the attitude of the central governments of the member states or the adoption of the Charter by the EC. But before this happens some fundamental questions will need to be addressed. For example, is it possible, even if desirable, to harmonize the legal framework of such widely differing authorities? Is it possible to focus on a legal concept such as general competence and attempt to harmonize, without also taking on the system of financial controls and all the other aspects of central–local relations? In regard to Britain, will it require external pressure to reverse the domination of central government, when internally it is only central government who can introduce such a change? There are also many other issues to be addressed, but perhaps most fundamental is that the challenge remains as to whether it is possible to harmonize institutional relationships in regard to principles which themselves demand diversity of response, or whether that very diversity will defeat the harmonization itself.

NOTES

This paper is a slightly revised version of that given to the Colloquium on Harmonisation and Legal Transplants, May 1991, University of Hamburg.

1. From the Explanatory Report, European Charter of Local Self-Government (1986), p. 9.
2. Michael Portillo, Minister for Local Government, UK (1990).
3. *Explanatory Report on the European Charter of Local Self-Government Strasbourg: Council of Europe 1986*. Also published in French under the title: *Rapport explicatif sur la Charte européenne de l'autonomie locale*.
4. *Hansard*, House of Lords, 31 Jan. 1991, col.792.
5. For a fuller explanation of this problem see M. Elliott, *The Role of Law in Central – Local Relations* (S.S.R.C, 1981) and M. Loughlin, *Local Government in the Modern State* (Sweet & Maxwell, 1986).
6. [1906] 1 Ch. 643.
7. [1943] 1 Ch. 86.
8. *Private Bills and New Procedures: A Consultation Document*, 1990, Cm. 1110.
9. *Hansard*, House of Lords, 31 Jan. 1991, col.792.
10. For a fuller analysis, see M. Clarke and J. Stewart, *Innovation in Local Government*, Local Government Training Board, 1989.
11. Peter Lodden, Coordinator, Ministry of Local Government, Norway in paper to Association of District Councils, February 1991.
12. M. Grant, 'The Case for Diversity in Local Government', report for the Local Authority Associations, 1991.

13. Widdicombe Committee, 'The Conduct of Local Authority Business', (1986) Cmnd. 9797. That report resulted in legislation including the Local Government and Housing Act 1989. See G. Ganz, 'The Depoliticisation of Local Government: The Local Government and Housing Act 1989. Part I', [1990] *Public Law* 224. Also, P. McAuslan, 'The Widdicombe Report: Local Government Business or Politics?', [1987] *Public Law* 154; M. Loughlin, 'The Conduct of Local Authority Business', [1987] *Modern Law Review* 64.
14. For example, the 'loan swaps' arrangements developed by the banks but declared unlawful by the House of Lords in *Hazell v. Hammersmith & Fulham L.B.C.* [1991] 1 All E.R. 545. For an excellent account of the issues and background see M. Loughlin, 'Innovative Financing in Local Government: The Limits of Legal Instrumentalism', [1990] *Public Law* 372.
15. Issued by the joint conference of the Association of County Councils, Association of District Councils, and Association of Metropolitan Authorities, 15 March 1991.
16. Committee on Structures Finance and Management, information document, 28 Feb. 1991.
17. Sir Duncan Lock, Vice-Chairman of the Committee on Structures, Finance and Mangement, Standing Conference of Local and Regional Authorities of Europe, May 1990.
18. M. Martins, 'Completing the Internal Market' in 'The Effects of 1992 on the Training of European Local and Regional Authority Staff', Working Paper 15 (1990), p. 14.
19. The Effects of 1992 on the Training of European Local and Regional Authority Staff, Working Paper 15 (1990), introductory report by Joan Hart, p. 12.

Index

accountability 10, 20, 21, 34–7, 80
administration 19, 20–25, 31–42, 48–9, 59–60
administrative powers 18, 21, 65
alderman 18–30
Attorney-General v. Manchester Corporation 73

Baden-Württemberg model 52–3
Banner, G. 52, 53
Blatch, Baroness 72, 76, 81
Brandenburg 46, 54–5
Britain 5–17, 69, 72–6, 79–81

cabinet system 11, 18–30
chief executive 45
citizens 38–41, 48, 52
city manager 12, 18–19, 22, 23, 28–9
committee system 6–9, 13–16
committees of local government 11–12, 13, 14, 20, 34–6, 60, 61–4
competence
  general 66, 71, 75, 76–7, 82
  ultra vires 74–5, 76, 77
constitution, municipal 29, 34–6, 44–6, 48, 50, 61
constitutional status of local governments 44–57, 70, 72–9
consultation 5–6
Council of Europe 69, 70
councillors 5–6, 7, 15

decision-making 8, 13–14, 23, 47–8, 59–61, 64
democracy 33, 46–8, 70

East Germany 46, 53–5, 57
Easton, David 38
Education Reform Act 1988 (UK) 78
effectiveness 37–8
efficiency 22, 31, 37–8, 48–9
election 5, 10, 11, 45, 47, 62
Erlander, Tage 34
European Charter of Local Self-Government 70–72, 81–4,
executive
  collective 7, 11, 12, 16, 20–23
  political 6, 7, 9–13, 16, 18–20, 59–68
  executive committees 34, 60, 61–4

finance
  constraint 38, 75, 76, 79, 80, 81
  management 27–8, 71
  taxation 38, 72, 79–81, 82

Germany 19, 44–57

Heseltine review, 77, 81

Internal Management of Local Authorities in England 5–6, 14, 16–17
Italy 59–68

Kunz-Zapf 52

leadership 8, 13–14, 16, 48, 52
Local Authority Act 142, 1990 (Italy) 61–7
Local Government Act 1933 (UK) 73
Local Government Act 1972 (UK) 75
Local Government Act 1977 (Sweden) 33
Local Government Act 1991 (Sweden) 36, 40
Local Government Finance Act 1982 (UK) 76
Local Government Finance Act 1988 (UK) 80
Local Government and Housing Act 1989 (UK) 8, 75, 78
Local Government Planning and Land Act 1980 (UK) 79
Local Government (Scotland) Act 1973 (UK) 75
Lock, Sir Duncan 71, 82
Lodden 78

managers 12, 22, 28–9, 67
mayor, 11, 18–19, 45, 47–8, 50, 52, 54, 63

Nassmacher 53
North Rhine-Westphalia 19, 44–57
Norway 18–30, 77–8

officials, powers and role of 64–8
Oslo 18–30

parliamentary system 19, 20, 21, 25–7
participation, political 39, 46–8
party groups 13, 41–2
party politics 7, 8, 22, 25–7, 33, 41, 47

political control 23-5, 34-7
Principles of Local Government 81
privatization 36, 40, 41-2
professionalization 32, 35, 49
professionals 10, 21-2, 25, 35, 45, 64
proportional representation 20, 63
public participation 32, 34, 38-40, 48, 52

Rates Act 1984 (UK) 79-80
reform
   administrative 13-16, 20-23, 31-5, 38, 39, 44-56, 59-60
   political 13-16, 33, 41-2
representation 46-7
Royal Commissions 74-5

Schramm 52
Scotland 73, 75
Sweden 31-42

unification (Germany) 46
user control 40

Wehling 53